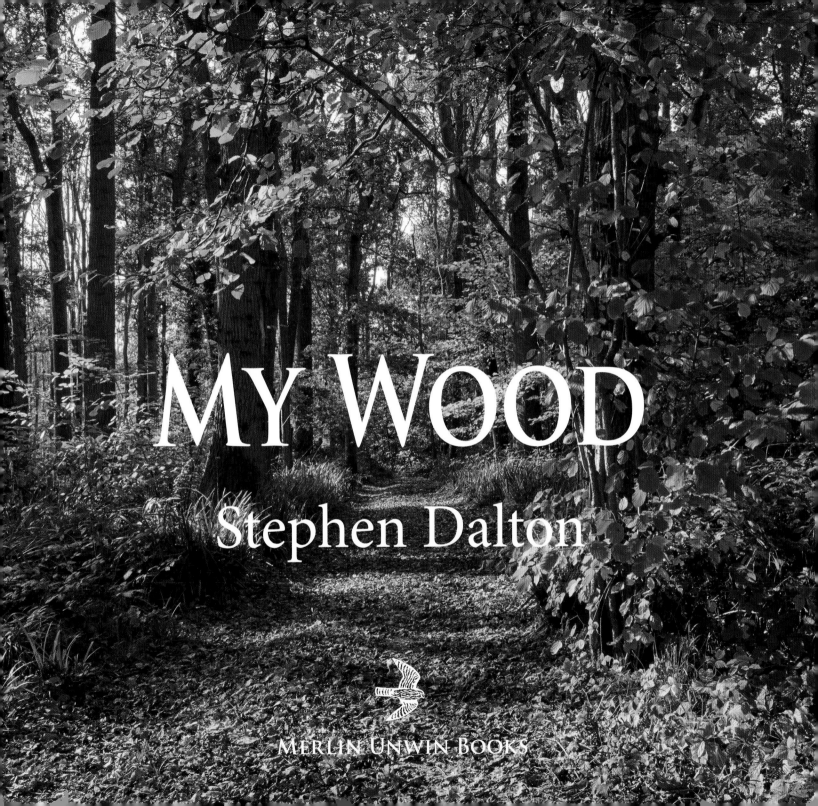

MY WOOD

Stephen Dalton

MERLIN UNWIN BOOKS

First published in Great Britain by Merlin Unwin Books Ltd, 2017

Text and photographs © Stephen Dalton, 2017

Merlin Unwin Books Ltd
Palmers House, 7 Corve Street, Ludlow
Shropshire SY8 1DB   UK

www.merlinunwin.co.uk

ISBN 978-1-910723-44-9

Typeset in 12 point Minion Pro by Merlin Unwin Books

Printed by Leo Paper Products

Acknowledgements

I would like to thank the publishers, Merlin and Karen for their enthusiasm during the book's three month production and for twisting my arm to write it in double quick time. Thanks also to my friends Philip Glyn and Evan Jones whose love of all living things is infectious.

Photo page iv: Wood mouse

CONTENTS

To my wife Liz
whose help and encouragement was invaluable – and for putting up
with my lack of patience with household matters during the hectic
time this book was being prepared

PREFACE

This book is not intended to be a showcase of nature photography, but a record of some of the wildlife and plants that depend on this small patch of woodland for their existence. Perhaps more than anything, I have tried to capture the spirit of the place, a place where nature can live and procreate without the threat of its habitat being destroyed – at least for the time being. It is also a place where I, my family and friends, can relax and gain spiritual enrichment in a 'real' world which is vanishing rapidly.

More locally, the book is a plea to save the countryside of Sussex, which is being destroyed exponentially by development of thousands of extra houses and their attendant infrastructure – all to satisfy a never-ending expansion of the human population in a small country.

About the Photography

Almost all the photographs in this book were taken in Rookery Wood within the last few years, using natural light, except for the high-speed flash images which, for complex technical reasons, had to be taken in my studio. Ten different cameras were employed to capture these images. Apart from spotting and dealing with minor blemishes and colour balance adjustments, digital manipulation has been avoided.

Stephen Dalton
June 2017

Man can't wait for the cooling of the world to consume everything in it, from teak trees to hummingbirds, and in a century or two hence will find himself perplexed by a planet in which there is nothing except what he makes.

The Spectator [1887]

INTRODUCTION

We purchase the farm

In the hot dry summer of 1976, the year when the countryside over much of Britain was looking parched, with drooping trees and brown desiccated lawns, my wife and I bought a little Victorian farm cottage in the heart of the Sussex Weald within an Area of Outstanding Natural Beauty.[1]

The surrounding farm was set among steep rolling hills, small fields and woodland. It was a ravishingly beautiful part of the Sussex Weald with extensive and distant views to the South Downs on clear days. The garden consisted of a half-acre patch of field that had been crudely wired off with a single strand of barbed wire. Like the rest of the countryside, the 'garden' was suffering from the most severe drought for many decades, the only greenery being a capacious growth of broad-leaved dock, a plant able to withstand droughts by sending its roots deep underground, so that the garden looked more like a field of cabbages than grass. The house too was no answer to a maiden's prayer but the surrounding airspace was alive with dozens of house martins, *Delichon urbicum*, which were nesting under the eaves.

There was hardly a building in sight and the timeless view was enhanced by attractive red-brown Sussex cattle that ambled around in the adjacent pastures.

Then, without warning, our tranquil life was threatened. The farm came up for sale. Developers and prospective chicken farmers began nosing around the land and adjacent buildings, with a view to purchase. We were now faced with the prospect of putting up with disturbance all round us or moving. After much soul-searching, we and our neighbours decided to buy the farm, our smaller portion consisting of 45 acres including cattle barns and some dilapidated stables close to the house – a solution that ensured that we could continue to be blessed with a spectacularly beautiful landscape – and the martins. Also there was the possibility of converting one of the barns into a photographic studio.

Most of the land was pasture so we rented out the fields to our friend Tom, the local farmer, for grazing his dairy cattle. Before dairy farmers were forced out of business towards the end of the 20th century[2], cows kept the grass under control, the livestock encouraging flies and other insects to breed, thereby helping to feed insectivorous birds such as swallows and martins. We banned the use of pesticides and herbicides and persuaded Tom to avoid the use of fertilisers as we hoped to reduce the fertility of the soil, in order to encourage wildflowers, and hence insects and other life that depend on flowering plants. In the fullness of time, hedges were planted together with a two hectare plantation of native trees on the edge of the largest and least inspiring field. Although the plan significantly improved the aesthetics of the landscape, what we failed to realise at this time was the looming menace of fallow deer, *Dama dama*.

Although we delighted in the responsibility of managing the pastures and new plantation in an eco-friendly manner, what the land sorely lacked was woodland. For me, woodlands and forests, whether temperate or tropical, are enchanting and spiritual places in which to spend time. By their very nature, woodland vegetation reigns, with trees large and small supporting a wealth of plant and animal life second to none. They also offer protection from the cold winds of winter, while during the hot summer months they are cool and refreshing. Indeed one of the many pleasures of entering woodlands during an uncomfortable hot summer's day is the escape into the shade where it is much cooler. In addition, the green canopy can significantly reduce the temperature through the process of transpiration.[3]

As you enter any forest, wildlife may not jump out at you, as there are so many places creatures can hide: high up in the canopy, low down under leaves, in or under fallen wood, in burrows or in thick shrubbery. Yet it is there, waiting to be discovered. Personally, I don't necessarily

Rainbow and cattle

When we acquired the farm in the late 1980s, most of the land consisted of pasture which we rented out to the local dairy farmer. This field is the largest and was a sea of dock, so naturally it was named Dockfield. We replaced any barbed wire boundary fences with hedges and planted a few specimen oak and cherry trees to create a more park-like setting, while over the following few decades the health of the soil gradually improved. Now it consists of fine grasses and a limited range of wild flowers which have managed to survive grazing animals. Avoiding the use of fertilisers, herbicides and insecticides and taking an annual crop of 'organic' hay and grazing a few cattle from time to time has worked wonders. Once more, the hedges act as wildlife corridors to Rookery Wood. Or they did, until the fallow deer started browsing on them.

Fallow resting in grassland

The source of the main problem faced by Rookery Wood. When present in excessive numbers, these appealing and innocent-looking 'bambies' will strip a wood of all growth under about a metre high, including wild flowers, tree shoots and saplings, ruining any chance of variety and interest in woods both small and large. This is a relatively small group resting in a field immediately adjacent to my wood – more often there are about sixty of them! The photograph was taken in late spring with blackthorn in full flower and the fresh pink leaves of walnut unfurling. You can see the 'browsing line' created by the deer along the hedge.

---

have to always see it, so long as I know it is there. Remaining still and quiet while looking and listening for rustles in the undergrowth or movement in the thickets will soon give the game away.

Entering an English oakwood during spring is obviously more immediately rewarding when it is accompanied by the glorious sound of bird song echoing all around, emerging spring

4

flowers and the fresh green haze of spring breaking through the trees. The only drawback to being immersed in so much beauty is the reminder of what we are losing, as well as what we've got.

Recent research suggests that entering established woodlands reduces blood pressure. Also it has been shown that trees release chemicals that somehow communicate to other trees. Maybe it's these substances, whatever they are, that have this effect on the blood pressure of humans. Perhaps a simpler and more logical explanation is that the mere act of entering beautiful places full of life and bird song with towering trees that reach to the heavens simply relaxes the mind and refreshes the spirit. Most likely it is a combination of the two.

An example of plant communication occurs in the thorn trees and bushes of Africa. When such a tree is attacked by an antelope or giraffe for instance, it produces unpalatable toxins in its leaves, so after a time the attacker abandons the bush. Instead of transferring its attention to an adjacent thorn, the animal wanders off upwind or 100 or so metres downwind beyond the reach of the toxin molecules which are also released into the air. In this way the volatile toxins released are 'smelled' by its immediate thorny neighbours which are thus fore-warned, so they too are stimulated to release toxins and become unpalatable. Here we have a communication mechanism among plants that protects not only the initial victim, but also potential victims in the immediate vicinity, thus sharing damage between a number of spaced trees. Other studies published in the 1980s on poplar and willow demonstrate that these plants warn one another when attacked by insects, triggering their release of volatile compounds, but how all this communication works is subject to a great deal of speculation.

It been shown that much communication takes place at root level when the trees encounter the roots of their neighbours. When trees are growing together in a forest, the stronger ones help out the weaker individuals, so those with less water, light or nutrients, are somehow compensated through an underground social network of roots ramifying throughout the forest. Perhaps this is not all that surprising when one considers that just as much, or more, of the tree is living below the ground as above. It seems that there is a form of electro-chemical communication that takes place between the roots, albeit far slower than that via the nerves of animals. Fungal hyphae also play a vital part in the health of trees and other plants. A recent study has shown that a teaspoonful of forest soil of an established wood contains miles of these microscopic 'fungal roots'. How the role of fungi operates in conjunction with green plants is the subject of much research.

We buy Rookery Wood at auction

As luck would have it, in 1998, ten years after acquiring the farmland, a nine-acre parcel of woodland[4] adjoining our land that I had hankered after for some time came up for auction. My wife and I attended the auction and after much competitive bidding, we managed to acquire it. We were now owners of an interesting little wood as well as half a farm!

At first glance the newly-acquired woodland appeared a boggy, brambly sedge-bound entanglement with an abundance of over-crowded ash trees, *Fraxinus excelsior,* and old straggly hazel *Corylus avellana,* but it became clear that with the right management such as felling and coppicing, it would make an interesting mini nature reserve. Already one of its most exciting features was the presence of a small rookery, one that over past years had provided us with endless pleasure from the birds' social interactions and evident enjoyment of flight whatever the weather. Naturally we re-named our new acquisition Rookery Wood.

Rookery Wood can be divided roughly into three areas. The lower part becomes increasingly steep as it approaches the bottom of the valley where it meets a steeply banked, meandering, fast-flowing stream. In spring, the banks are embellished with a profuse growth of wild garlic, *Allium ursinum,* and a sparse sprinkling of bluebells, *Hyacinthoides non-scripta*, and yellow archangels or yellow dead-nettle, *Lamium galeobdolon,* while further up is a stretch of blackthorn *Prunus spinosa*, which was beginning to show signs of deer damage. The area is further distinguished by

---

A drone's eye view of Rookery Wood *right*

An aerial view of the entire wood clearly showing its peninsular form and its relationship with the surrounding fields. The large piece of woodland to which it is attached extends a couple of miles in both directions, a little brook separating the two. Apart from large trees, this chunk of surrounding woodland is pitifully barren of meaningful plants and wildlife as a result of the huge uncontrolled fallow population.

Trees are majestic beings under whose canopy we are as insignificant as ants. This small patch of woodland which is Rookery Wood defies its nine acre size by its biodiversity, as it has been protected from the appalling damage wrought by massive herds of fallow deer by a two metre-high fence. In spite of being erected only a few years ago, the plant and wildlife within its boundary is far richer than the hundreds of acres of surrounding woodland, although the dramatic difference can only be appreciated by strolling through both.

about 200 foot high Wellingtonia-like Japanese cedars *Cryptomeria japonica*. These are popular with 'our' buzzards, *Buteo buteo*, which have nested here on more than one occasion. I suspect ravens *Corvus corax* may have also nested in one of these trees recently. Until about thirty years ago, these impressive and intelligent birds were only seen in the West Country and Scotland, but now ravens can be spotted or heard flying over Rookery Wood almost daily. The mere sound of their deep croak enriches our day.

The mid-portion of the wood is dominated by a thick stand of ash, which after about a hundred years of growth, and being overcrowded, are tall and straight with little or no lower foliage. Over the years we have been thinning these out to allow more light through to the forest floor, benefiting both the ground flora and our wood-burning stove, providing the latter with an almost inexhaustible supply of logs. The only plants that thrived at ground level were pendulous sedge, *Carex pendula*, and dog's mercury, *Mercurialis perennis* – almost all other plants having been crucified by fallow deer. Nowadays, deer have no natural predators so with each succeeding year their numbers increase. When we bought the land about thirty years ago, we only encountered the odd band of half a dozen or so – now we regularly disturb herds of 70 plus, but thanks to our deer fencing, Rookery Wood is now fully protected and the bramble is returning.

The top zone of the woodland is the most attractive and the nearest thing to ancient woodland. Higher up the slope, the wood here is drier and there are several large oaks, *Quercus robur,* and ash, accompanied by old straggly hazel in desperate need of coppicing. During spring, the floor is covered with a thick carpet of bluebells intermingled with other plants including dog's mercury, Enchanter's nightshade, *Circaea lutetiana,* and yellow archangel, while a white suffusion of blackthorn blossom monopolizes its lower regions as it merges with the mid area. The top zone is also the province of the rooks, *Corvus frugilegus,* which nest in the tops of the mature ash trees.

---

[1] Designated areas of outstanding natural beauty (AONBs) in England are outside national parks and yet are considered to have such natural beauty that it is desirable they are conserved and enhanced.
[2] From the 1980s farmers in UK were gradually forced out of business by supermarket price-cutting and crazy European CAP regulations
[3] Transpiration is the process whereby water is carried from the roots to pores on the underside of leaves where it evaporates into the atmosphere. An increase in temperature warms the water in the leaves, causing more evaporation and a corresponding cooling effect.
[4] The terms woodland and forest are often used synonymously but there is a difference. Woodlands are generally smaller and have areas where sunlight is abundant while forests are often darker with overlapping crowns. Plantations managed for timber production (forestry) are usually referred to as forests.

Rookery Wood with bluebells

The upper end of Rookery Wood, which is much drier than the lower region, supports a healthy growth of bluebells. Because it has a number of large oak and ash, together with a few indicator plants such as dog's mercury, wild garlic and wood spurge, it is nearest to being ancient woodland.

The photograph was taken in mid-April before the ash had broken into leaf, while the oak was just starting to leaf up with its characteristic warm-coloured foliage of fresh leaves and opening buds.

A few rook's nests are visible in the upper branches of the large ash trees.

NOTE: This introduction describes the state of the property at about the time we took it over. The next section will outline steps taken to improve access to all areas; the creation of rides; the felling of trees to allow more light penetration; extending the range of different vegetation heights by coppicing, strimming and providing small glades and a greater variety to edges. Such steps are vital to encourage a wider range of plant and animal life.

At a later stage a more ambitious project was the creation of a woodland pond. Finally there will be an explanation for our failure to realise the impending impact of the population explosion of fallow deer, and our somewhat abortive attempts to reduce the appalling damage they wrought – and the final solution.

SPRING

NOWADAYS February often heralds the arrival of spring, that most bewitching time of the year. After weeks of long, cold and dreary January days, nothing lifts one's spirit more than the ringing tones of a mistle thrush, *Turdus viscivorus,* echoing around Rookery Wood – its alternative name 'storm cock' reflecting its readiness to sing in a heavy storm. This optimistic bird seems to sense spring is on the way before we do, even when the weather appears grim to us. By mid-February when finally the sun manages to break through the gloom, various tits may join in the chorus, confirming that spring really has arrived, but it's also a reminder that our climate is warming.

Bright yellow hazel catkins are out and the vivid green tips of bluebell leaves are breaking between and through the fallen oak leaves. On damper days, small clouds of winter gnats perform their courtship dances hovering above any bright areas in shafts of sunlight. Nature is in the process of awakening and the world seems a brighter place. Walking down a sunny woodland ride is the perfect place to be at this time, particularly as the trees and shrubs offer protection from the north or easterly February winds. Out in the open fields, spring seems less welcoming.

One of the first flowers to appear in early spring is the opposite-leaved golden saxifrage. Mats of this bright green flower can be seen wherever it is sufficiently moist such as the banks of streams and ditches, making the mid and lower regions of Rookery Wood ideal for this plant. Another flower that favours a moist place is lady's smock or cuckoo flower; it appears shortly after the saxifrage and is the food plant of the orange tip butterfly. Growing in the drier areas are clumps of the ubiquitous primrose, violets and a single small patch of wood anemones.

There are only two species of orchids found in the wood: one is the common spotted orchid which pops up in odd places now and again; and the other is the early purple orchid which reliably appears each year in one shady spot, but how it has managed to survive the attacks of rabbits and deer over the last decade or two is a mystery.

A particularly distinctive but common flower dotted around the wood is wood spurge. Growing up to 60cm high with small glowing yellow-green flowers and leaves tinged with purple, this plant can hardly fail to attract attention, perhaps even more so when the complex flowers are

examined close-up. The central zone of Rookery Wood is dominated by pendulous sedge, a thick leathery thug of a plant which prospers anywhere where the ground is damp. Unfortunately its invasive growth prevents more interesting and insect-attracting flowering plants to gain a foothold.

Pendulous sedge

One of the more intractable dilemmas of Rookery Wood is managing the vigorous growth of pendulous sedge which dominates much of the central area. Its monoculture of thick growth smothers out any other plant that attempts to grow here. But since we felled much of the ash and erected the deer fence, bramble, a far more wildlife-friendly plant, is beginning to gain a footing at the expense of the sedge.

During spring, the sedge is in full flower, its copious quantity of pollen wafting through the wood when disturbed by either animals or wind.

Bogbean in flower

I had intended to be purist by letting nature establish herself in her own time, but impatience got the better of me when it came to this plant and to fish, both of which I introduced into Rookery Pond. The bogbean, *Menyanthes trifoliata*, as well as having comely white flowers tinged with pink in spring, also provides perfect cover for water birds and for aquatic insect nymphs to climb. The 3-spined stickleback should help to keep kingfishers happy, yet are small enough not to damage the invertebrate population unduly.

It is no surprise that a woodland pond supports certain specialised flowers such as marsh marigold or kingcups, *Caltha palustris,* which grow in clumps around the water's edge, a plant that attracts various tiny beetles and flies. Bogbean, *Menyanthes trifoliata,* too comes into flower about now, which although not confined to woodland ponds thrives well here in the shallow water.

Finally, but by no means least, are the hosts of bluebells that dominate the higher and drier parts of Rookery Wood. There can be few floral displays on earth that compare with our bluebell woods in late spring, filling the woodland floor with colour and the air with scent. What's more, insects, especially bumblebees, love them – as do all visitors who set foot here at this stunning time.

The sounds of spring are as uplifting as the sights. Among the earliest are the sounds of the nuthatch and greater-spotted woodpecker, both of which nest in Rookery Wood every year. At about the same time, in early March, the courtship croaks of frogs and toads resonate around the water, the spawn being laid in the shallows well before the end of the month. At the same time it is impossible to ignore the clamorous voices of nesting rooks which echo throughout the wood and well beyond; later these will be boosted by the impatient calls of their young demanding to be fed. As much as I love the sound of happy rooks, there are times when the cacophony subsides and is replaced by the glorious songs of smaller birds such as thrushes, blackbirds, chaffinches, robins, wrens and – one of my favourite songbirds – the blackcap. Spring song is what many of us nature

Opposite-leaved golden saxifrage

A particularly attractive, if sometimes overlooked little plant is the opposite-leaved golden saxifrage *Chrysosplenium oppositifolium*. The shady and wet parts of Rookery Wood are the perfect habitat for it. Mats of this moss-like flower first appear in March, brightening up seeping wet spots around ditches and streams with its vivid green and golden foliage.

lovers have been waiting for over the last nine months, connecting us to the natural world in a way few other experiences can match.

A few of these birds such as the chiffchaffs and blackcaps have flown halfway round the world to return to their probable birthplace in Rookery Wood. But the greylag geese that nest here have flown from somewhere much closer to home, because unlike other geese, they are resident in UK. When they arrive they tend to swim around rather furtively in search of a suitable nesting site which they always choose on the larger of the two islands. When incubating in April, they are almost impossible to spot: not only do they keep stock still but their coloration provides perfect camouflage with the island's mixed vegetation. There are a pair of resident moorhens that usually nest on the same little island but on the opposite side. One bird incubates while the other skulks around on the surface, eating pond weed or hiding amidst the verdant growth at the pond margins.

When the weather is warm enough, a gentle stroll around the pond's perimeter is always rewarding, whether it's watching a bee fly probing the nectaries of a primrose or bugle; or a hoverfly basking in the sun on a log or patch of dry ground; or perhaps agile wolf spiders running around the dry fallen oak leaves. In the water, huge clumps of frog spawn lie heaped up in the shallows; and strings of toad spawn are twined up amidst the aquatic plants below. In some places, tiny three-spined stickleback can be spotted swimming leisurely around, taking advantage of the warmer shallows – fodder for the kingfisher when they mature. If you are lucky, a soft rustling in the ground vegetation betrays a grass snake as it slithers away to safety or a puzzling ripple on the water surface is most likely to be one swimming across the pond from one bank to the other. Dragonflies are not on the wing until the end of April or early June: the first species likely to be seen is the large red damselfly, an insect that prefers well-vegetated places close to water, Rookery Wood being ideal. Azure damsel flies and the larger species emerge from their nymphal stage later in May or June. Both of these insect jewels spend much time basking at the water's edge, but as soon as the sun disappears, they too mysteriously vanish.

The first butterfly on the wing here is likely to be a lone red admiral, *Vanessa atalanta,* (below) or a peacock, *Aglais io,* that has woken up from hibernation, but occasionally a brimstone, *Gonepteryx rhamni,* turns up, a butterfly that always seems to be in a hurry. Since the larva's nearest foodplant, the alder buckthorn, is about half a kilometre away, it is always a bonus to see this bright sulphur-yellow butterfly dashing through Rookery Wood. Then as spring gets fully underway, the orange-tip butterfly, *Anthocharis cardamines,* emerges after over-wintering as a chrysalis and dances down the rides in search of lady's smock to lay its eggs, a flower which it shares with the most prolific butterfly in Rookery Wood, the green-veined white. Summer is well on its way now.

A common toad emerges from hibernatory shelter

Peering out of its daytime retreat from under a tree stump, a common toad, *Bufo bufo,* seems unconcerned by a fly landing on its nose. Their favourite food includes slugs, snails, spiders and ants which they catch with their thick chameleon-like tongues.

When breeding, the toads congregate around their favourite ponds, including Rookery Pond, and after mating they move away from the water to resume their solitary lifestyle on dry land.

Hazel and catkins

The wood contains at least 150 hazel trees in its shrub layer. Some are old and dying as a consequence of not being coppiced for at least 50 years, while those that have been recently coppiced have taken on a new lease of life. Hazel trees can reach a height of over thirty feet and live up to 80 years unpruned or several hundred if coppiced.

As well as providing winter food for mammals such as squirrels, wood mice and dormice, hazel is a popular food plant for a wide range of insects including beetles and moth larvae. Their familiar male flowers, catkins, hang in clusters during February, while the female flowers are tiny bud-like arrangements with red styles.

Nuthatch hunting insects

This dapper little bird, *Sitta europaea*, is more often heard than seen. Its wide range of loud and rapid calls echo around the wood almost every day in spring or early summer. Nuthatches are omnivorous, feeding on insects, nuts and seeds. They nest in existing holes in trees and walls, often reducing the size of the holes by plastering them up with mud.

A muntjac grazes the native bluebells

Muntjac, or Barking Deer, of which there are several species, are the oldest known deer in the world, with remains found in Miocene deposits from Europe. The Reeves Muntjac, *Muntiacus reevesi,* occurs naturally in the Far East but those in Britain originally escaped from Woburn Abbey estate around 1925. They are diminutive and furtive creatures which can rapidly eliminate woodland flowers, saplings and fresh coppiced growth in a small wood, and unlike most other deer species, they breed at a rapid rate at any time of the year.

Muntjac are most active at night, but the single individual here that has been living happily in the wood since the fence was erected, can sometimes be found wandering around in the middle of the day.

Here it is caught by a trail camera amongst the bluebells. Although these animals will damage bluebells, a single individual shouldn't cause too much havoc amongst this sea of blue!

Bluebells

The beauty of bluebells is not merely in the flowers themselves but in the glorious woodland settings in which they grow. A scene of exquisite beauty like this, vibrant with scent, bird song and the hum of insects, triumphs over man's never-ending destruction of life and beauty in the name of development and progress.

Top end of Rookery Wood with bluebells
right

The upper, drier end of Rookery Wood is the best area for bluebells. They start blooming well before the tree canopy fully develops, and by the middle of May when the leaves unfold and cast shadows over the woodland floor, the more shade-tolerant flowers appear such enchanter's nightshade *Circaea lutetiana* and dog's mercury *Mercurialis perennis*

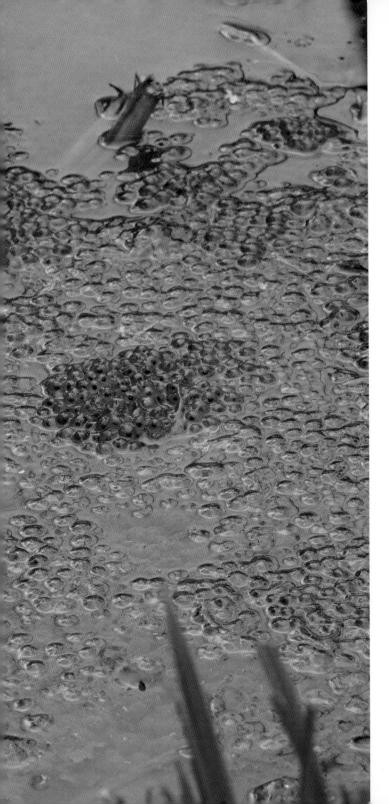

Frog spawn

There is a large population of frogs and toads living in the wood, and the pond provides the perfect habitat for them to mate and spend their immature stages. Early spring is the time to find the huge rafts of spawn of the common frog *Rana temporaria* accumulating in the shallow regions of the water.

Later in the season when the adults leave for drier land, the numerous streams, ditches and moist patches and the surrounding thick vegetation continue to provide these amphibians with a perfect habitat during their mature years.

Violets *left*

The term dog violet refers to a number of species of scentless violets, this one probably being the most common, *Viola riviana*. The flower can be seen carpeting many of the rides in Rookery Wood during spring and early summer. Its most important role here is to supply food for the larvae of the silver-washed fritillary – a good reason for keeping the rides under control.

Wood spurge *right*

Wood spurge, *Euphorbia amygdaloides*, is characteristic of old damp woods so naturally it thrives well here. It is a tall plant with reddish leaves that spiral around the stem and the splendid yellow-green leaves make it impossible to confuse with any other woodland plant. Like all spurges, the male and female blooms are separate, a ring of male flowers surrounding each female one.

Wood anemonies *top left*

The wood anemone, *Anemone nemorosa*, is very much a woodland plant but only a small patch survives in Rookery Wood. It is a characteristic plant of ancient woodland, appearing at about the same time as the primrose. On cold, dull days the flowers close and droop to protect the pollen, and dance when there is any sign of a breeze. Hence, the flower is also known as the windflower – Edward Elgar, a lover of the countryside, named his special friend and admirer Alice Stuart Wortley 'Windflower'.

English bluebell *top right*

Bluebells, brimstones and birdsong – all three come together in April, helping to make spring the most magical time of the year. The English bluebell is a delight to behold, but Spanish bluebells are now invading our woodlands – these are larger more gaudy and blousy than our more subtle native species. Unfortunately the two are cross breeding forming a tough hybrid which is not good news for our woodlands.

Spring activity in the rookery

There has been a thriving rookery here ever since I can remember and the various corvine activities are a source of interest throughout the year. Spring is a particularly busy time for the rooks – having devoted the last month or so to constructing or repairing their nests of sticks, the birds are now constantly flying in and out of the wood to collect food for their small young.

This colony is so much part of our lives that it is almost impossible not to venture outside without hearing their raucous calls or seeing them in the sky or surrounding fields.

American signal crayfish

This formidable-looking creature, the American signal crayfish, *Pasifastacus leniusculus,* poses a serious threat to the native wildlife of rivers, ponds and lakes, and particularly to our now much rarer native species, the white-clawed crayfish. The alien was introduced to Britain in the 1970s, and is one of the many introductions of alien animals and plants such as the grey squirrel and Japanese knotweed that have proved a dreadful mistake. Unfortunately the little brook at the bottom of the woodland valley is now infested with these crustaceans which burrow into the banks at or below water level. Not only does this result in collapsing banks and soil run-off, but these animals eat our smaller native crayfish species as well as the rest of the aquatic fauna. The signal crayfish can wander a considerable distance across land to invade ponds and water courses in fresh territories.

This large individual was discovered in a field by my son while out walking; it was possibly on the way to invade Rookery Pond. Armed with the tip-off, I followed with a camera and took this photograph. Clearly the creature did not approve of my presence!

Courting toads

During March the pond is bubbling and croaking with the courting activities of common toads *Bufo bufo* in their long and rather hectic efforts to secure mates. These amphibians converge on the pond from all over the wood and beyond to breed here. In their struggle to secure mates, many males may attach themselves to a single female, resulting in a sprawling mass of bodies with the unfortunate female stuck in the middle.

The mating embrace of a toad is known as amplexus, fertilisation of the eggs taking place externally. Unlike frog spawn, toad spawn is wrapped around aquatic vegetation in long double helix chains of some 7,000 eggs.

Azure damselfly

Dragonflies are at the top of my favourite insect list and a sure sign that spring has arrived is when these winged jewels appear in fight. The first to emerge is the large red damselfly, followed closely by the azure damselfly *Coenagrion puella*. It is the most common damselfly to be seen around the pond and in the clearings beyond.

Damselflies are smaller and more delicately-built than dragonflies, have a more fluttering flight, and they normally rest their wings held together over their backs rather than stretched out to the side.

Primroses *above*

The humble primrose is an authentic woodland flower that thrives in hedgerows, damp banks, glades and coppiced woodland. The bright splashes of yellow scattered around Rookery Wood are especially welcome before the green foliage opens, never failing to lift the spirits on a sunny spring morning.

Wild daffodills *right*

The yellow trumpets of wild daffodils, *Narcissus pseudonarcissus,* is enough the brighten up the dullest of spring days, their two-toned yellow distinguishing them from the garden varieties. It is always a surprise to come across a host of these popular flowers while strolling in the dappled shade of an ancient woodland. They are most prolific in the West Country and Wales but Holly Farm is fortunate in having a bank of them hidden away in a remote pasture as well as a small cluster growing in the wood close to the pond. Due to loss of habitat, this flower has declined significantly during the 19th century.

The wood from afar

A view of Rookery Wood in spring from across the fields on a typical April day. The foreground pasture is a rich green, full of nourishment for any grazing animal. Whereas the hawthorn 'corridor' hedge has already greened up, the wood still looks dark as the ash has yet to open. The yellow-green leaves of fresh oak can be seen easily from some distance away.

Kingcups

During spring and early summer the water's edge is decked with a wide variety of water-loving flowering plants including patches of kingcups or marsh marigold, *Caltha palustris*, whose brilliant yellow flowers attract all sort of flies, beetles and small moths. The flower is widespread in watery and boggy places in both wooded and open habitats. It is a close relative of the buttercup and the whole plant is poisonous to grazing animals.

The pond in May

By mid May most of the wood is a sea of lush greenery, impenetrable in parts due to the thickets of blackthorn and bramble which have held sway since the exclusion of fallow deer. In the foreground, yellow flag, water dropwort, reed mace, willow herb and pendulous sedge are all springing into life on this low boggy peninsular.

Greater pondweed *Potamogeton natans* has taken over much of the pond surface.

Dandelions

The dandelion *Teraxacum officinale* is a ubiquitous flower if ever there was one, but with an intriguingly beautiful seed head with designer seeds.

Early Purple Orchid

The woodland-loving early purple orchid, *Orchis mascula*, is one of the earliest flowering spring orchids, first appearing in April. It used to be common but due to the same old story of development and 'improved' farming practice to make way for the burgeoning human population, this flower is nothing like as common as it once was.

Fortunately there is a small patch in a lower region of the wood growing alongside dog's mercury and a few bluebells. They seem to struggle to exist here as each year they are nibbled by rabbits or slugs.

Recently, to protect them from mammals, I've surrounded the remaining specimens with a wire fence.

Badger foraging among the bluebells

This badger picture was specially taken for the book, but not before at least six weeks of frustration. Since the fencing was done, badgers and foxes have always managed to gain access to Rookery Wood simply by burrowing under the heavy-gauge wire – badgers are exceedingly difficult to exclude from anywhere as they operate like giant moles. But this has never been a problem as the only seriously unwelcome guests here are the deer. Indeed my trail cameras prove that both badgers and foxes roam around the wood every night – that is until I decided to try for a high quality photograph specifically for this book, rather than a fuzzy trail camera image! Then, for some unaccountable reason, the animals suddenly decided to abandon the place. There was no point in going through all the hassle of setting up weather-proof infra-red sensors, several flash units and a camera capable of producing high quality images, on a badger trail where there were zero badgers.

Finally my luck changed when the trail cameras revealed resumed activity by these recalcitrant creatures. The only explanation I can think of for their absence is the long period of dry weather that the country has been 'enjoying', when the clay-rich ground has been like concrete and the badgers' favourite prey, slugs and snails, were not active at night. So after six weeks of fretting, and a few days before the publisher's deadline, I managed to obtain this photograph.

Oak shoot

An oak seedling sprouts from a grassy patch on the woodland floor. Over the next few hundred years it has to survive all manner of threats including rabbits, the solitary muntjac (in this wood) and trampling human feet before it develops into a hundred-foot tree.

Lady's smock or Cuckoo flower *right*

Lady's smock, *Cardamine pratensis*, is also known as the cuckoo flower because it coincides with the arrival of the first cuckoo. Fortunately, though, it is far more common than the bird. Much loved, this flower has been a symbol of emerging spring for country folk and poets alike for centuries. The white-to-pale pink flower is a common feature in damp grassland, banks and open woodland including Rookery Wood. It is one of the food plants of the orange-tip butterfly.

Bee fly feeding from bugle

Bee flies *Bombyliidae* are on the wing at the same time as primroses and bugles are blooming and seem to be particularly plentiful in Rookery Wood during early spring. Bee flies hover over flowers, often resting their front legs on the flower lip while they suck the nectar with their very long and permanently extended proboscis. The larvae are parasitic on the larvae of solitary bees and wasps, the adult female flicking her eggs towards the entrance of the underground nests.

The track of a foraging snail *above*

Like all molluscs, slugs do not possess conventional mandibles, or teeth. Instead they have a specialised rasping organ called a radula, which resembles a bucket wheel excavator, with special muscles for operating it. As they trundle along eating, they leave a characteristic pattern in their wake which is particularly clear after moving over a flat, algae-covered surface.

Thrush's anvil *left*

A few years ago I found a flat stone in one of the woodland rides which was being used as a thrush's anvil. It was used by a song thrush *Turdus philomelos* for smashing open snail shells to access the snail's soft body. It is clear from the numerous broken shells scattered all around that this anvil was much in demand – the picture was taken in April when the thrush was at its busiest, feeding fledglings. As can be seen from the fragments, the most common snail in my wood is the banded snail *Cepaea*.

47

Grass snake

Grass snakes *Natrix natrix* come in various shades of olive green, are long and tapering and normally have a yellow collar, all of which characteristics show well in this photograph and help to distinguish it from the adder. Just occasionally both species turn out black, in which case their shape should give the game away.

Unlike the adder which favours drier habitats, grass snakes prefer to live around the borders of woods and hedgerows, often close to water, so Rookery Wood would be perfect for them, but for the predatory activities of the regular visits from herons.

Grass snakes are excellent swimmers and can be seen from time to time swimming across the pond, a tell-tale trail of ripples following in their wake.

Long-tailed tit

A party of long-tailed tits, *Aegithalos caudatus,* gaily bouncing around a tree or bird feeder is always a pleasure to watch.

These birds are regular visitors to the wood as not only is there plenty of food but also no end of thick, thorny places amidst the blackthorn and wild rose in which to build their elasticised spider-web and feather domed nests.

Swarming tadpoles

Each year in April hundreds of thousands of toad and frog tadpoles swim in massive shoals all around the pond, keeping close to the surface, but why is not clear. It seems that they may be stimulated into activity by the warming water in the shallower regions, or maybe the tactic is a means of avoiding predators, in the same way that some other members of the animal kingdom band together to evade or confuse enemies.

Long-legged fly

Long-legged flies, *Dolychopodidae*, are a group of small flies that have a similar lifestyle to that of the larger robber flies, preying on tiny insects. Most species have long ungainly-looking legs while some have beautiful metallic-green bodies.

This species, like many others in the family, live in wet habitats around the margins of ponds and streams and have an elaborate courtship display, waving their wings about in a flag-like manner.

Speckled wood

In spite of its understated colour and indifferent flight, the speckled wood, *Pararge aegeria,* always lifts my spirits. It turns out, surprisingly, to be a bit of a tyrant, chasing off any other butterflies that dare to infringe its territory.

This butterfly loves woodlands, especially those blessed with dappled sunlit spots, where it is perfectly camouflaged; sometimes the butterfly lands at my feet or on a nearby leaf in a patch of sunlight before dashing off in pursuit of an intruder, only to return again to the same spot.

Most years see several pairs of these butterflies in Rookery Wood where they never fail to add charm to the place.

Stream with wild garlic

The brook at the bottom of the wood marks the boundary between Rookery Wood and our neighbour's land. For most of the year the banks leading down to the water are more or less barren due to the deer but during spring the whole area is transformed into a sea of green and white and a heavy aroma of garlic fills the air. Thankfully, wild garlic is one of the few plants that fallow ignore.

The brook still supports a few brown trout and a number of interesting and relatively unusual insects that have managed to avoid the rapacious menace of the American signal crayfish, *Pacifastacus leniusculus* (see page 30).

SUMMER

〰〰〰〰〰〰〰〰〰〰〰〰

ROOKERY WOOD is quieter in summer. Bird song is more subdued and even the calls of rooks are more restrained, now that most of the fledglings have left their nests. The magic of spring, with the warm colours of unfurling leaves has given way to colder greens, while in the glades and rides the sparkle of dew and threads of beaded gossamer are barely visible[1]. Spring flowers are giving way to summer flowers such as knapweed, enchanter's nightshade, gypsywort, hemp agrimony, and shrubby plants like wild rose and blackberry, so popular with emerging butterflies.

Dappled shade covers much of the woodland floor and the overriding sound is the soporific hum of bees and hoverflies. The courtship activities of birds are almost over, and caring for the young is now more important. Thanks to the fence and the on-going felling and coppicing regime, thick vegetation has sprung up in many places, especially around the pond, attracting many birds that were absent or scarce here before. As well as the usual blackbirds, song thrushes, robins and wrens, there are now long-tailed tits, chiffchaff, several pairs of blackcaps and the occasional bullfinch breeding here. All have been provided with nesting sites in the thickets of blackthorn and bramble and a consequential abundance of insect and plant food.

Mid summer is also the time when the silver-washed fritillaries and white admirals emerge. These impressive, fast and erratic-flying butterflies provide us with enormous pleasure as they dart around the rides and glades, dashing and gliding from one patch of bramble blossom to the next in their hunt for nectar or mates. In July I spend much time watching the activities of these alluring butterflies: one moment they are gently flying low over shrubbery, then in the next second they shoot out of sight into the tree canopy.

Unlike some of our gaudier species, these two have a hint of subtlety to their colouring – the fritillary's mosaic of black and orange-brown on the topside giving way to a suffusion of silver and jade green which comes into view as soon as it closes its wings. Then, if one's luck is in, swooping down from up high, the far-from-white, white admiral lands on a bramble flower a metre or two away – a magical moment. The upper wings of a freshly-emerged specimen are usually a matt black with a bar of brilliant white, a colour scheme which makes them difficult to spot in the harsh sunlight. Birds clearly find them tricky to catch, as often they have large niches pecked out of their wings.

White Admiral

Of all the butterflies that inhabit or visit Rookery Wood, the white admiral *Limenitis camilla* is my favourite, and I never fail to be moved on the few occasions I see one here. The exquisite flight of this velvety black and brown butterfly is a hard act to follow as it dashes off at breathtaking speed, or glides down on outstretched wings from the tree canopy – a sight to behold and the highlight of any midsummer visit to the wood.

The Large White

This butterfly is the notorious large 'cabbage' white *Pieris brassicae* which can be such a pest in vegetable gardens. On the few occasions that a large white visits Rookery Wood, this butterfly's behaviour is very different from the more common and prettier green-veined white, preferring to charge around the wood with its floppy flight on a tour of inspection with few stops. This one though obligingly paused to feed on a foxglove before resuming its restless flight.

Older specimens tend to become scruffy due to bramble damage, around which they spend so much of their lives. The blend of mature trees merging with the sunlight of the rides and glades is a perfect habitat for these two butterfly gems. While the adults feast on the free-flowing nectar of blackberry, and wild rose, the fritillary caterpillars munch on the violets that carpet the open spaces, and those of the white admiral favour clumps of honeysuckle that climb around trees and stumps.

Other butterflies too are flourishing. Green-veined whites are particularly common in Rookery Wood and I have counted up to ten at one time skipping about in the large central glade. Meadow browns and gatekeepers are also frequent feeders on the bramble and other flowering plants, although the latter generally prefer the open pastures at the woodland edges. Large and small skippers (*Large Skipper photo on page 57*) find their way to the few grassy patches where there are patches of bird's-foot trefoil, the food plant of their larvae. One of my favourite woodland butterflies is the speckled wood which prefers the shadier regions, thriving wherever the sun finds its way into a small glade or sunlit patch. Like the robin, these butterflies always seem to be chasing one another in territorial skirmishes.

Other less common species are the peacocks, red admiral and comma. The latter tends to confine itself to a small area where the same individual hangs around week after week. Unfortunately I have yet to see a small tortoiseshell in Rookery Wood in spite of the presence of numerous beds of nettles, their food plant. This butterfly used to be one of the most common species found in Britain but its numbers have dramatically dwindled over the recent years, probably due to parasites and the greenhouse effect.[2]

Activity on Rookery Pond never ceases during the warmer weather. An intriguing spectacle during early summer is the tadpole parade, when massive rivulets of the little amphibians swim around the pond: in some years there could be well over one hundred thousand of them swimming in meandering shoals, sometimes appearing to encircle the whole pond. Some develop into frogs, but the majority are common toad tadpoles, as early in the season this pond attracts adult toads from far and wide. Later in summer when the toadlets develop four legs, they vacate the water for dry land when it becomes nearly impossible to avoid treading on the little animals.

The moorhens which nest on the pond every year are scuttling around the surface feeding their 4-5 fluffy offspring which trail behind in their efforts to penetrate the thick growth of giant pond weed[3]. Moorhens are among the most shy birds I know, disappearing from view at the first sign of humans. It is extraordinary how they manage to hide amidst the most scanty foliage at the water's edge. Herons are disturbed almost every day, as this pond provides them with a rich source of prey including frogs, toads, newts, stickleback and sadly the occasional grass snake. At night one roosts in an old oak close to the water's edge.

Kingfishers are regular visitors during the summer and autumn months. On one memorable occasion I was watching a kingfisher fishing while a pair of silver-washed fritillaries were courting

Comma butterfly

The comma *Polygonnia c-album* is a woodland butterfly which I have always found endearingly affable, occasionally landing on one's arm or even head. The comma tends to keep to a restricted territory, returning to the same spot day after day. Each season the large central glade is the best place to find it. Like the peacock, brimstone and red admiral, after feeding up on nectar in late autumn the comma enters hibernation.

all around it. Two other water birds that nest here regularly are mallards and greylag geese, both species nesting on one or other of the two little islands, although the goslings never survive the fox for more than a few days.

The pond acts as a magnet for insects and spiders. The total dragonfly count is eleven species although their abundance varies significantly each year. The large red damselfly is the first to be spotted in spring, then as the days get warmer, some of the larger dragonflies appear on the wing in late May or June such as the rather infrequent metallic green downy emerald (*Cordulia aenea*) and perhaps the most magnificent of our dragonflies, the emperor. Other large dragonflies such as the brown and southern hawkers emerge a little later. Sometimes on a hot summer's day all three of these aerial dragons may be seen flying over the water together where there are frequent territorial disputes with audible clashing of wings. Caddisflies, alderflies and mayflies that spend their early stages in water are also reasonably common during summer; then there is a multitude of other insects including mosquitoes, midges and empid flies that generally fly close to water surface and pond edges.

Where there are insects there are spiders, and Rookery Wood is blessed with a number of interesting and quite scarce species. As well as several large orb weavers such as the marbled orb weaver (*Araneus marmoreus*) and the angular orb weaver (*Araneus angulatus*), the pond also champions the rarely-noticed ray spider (*Theridiosoma gemmosum*). This pin-head sized spider is nearly impossible to spot[4] but astonishingly it attaches the lower supporting struts of its web to the water surface, behaviour first observed on this very pond by my colleague Evan Jones[5]. Such wealth of invertebrate life provides excellent fodder for all manner of other creatures such as small birds, dragonflies – and bats. Up to half a dozen of these fascinating and skilled mammalian aeronauts can be seen any warm evening during summer hunting high and low above the water, feeding on the bountiful supply of small insects. When it becomes too dark to actually spot them, a bat detector picks out their ultrasonic calls almost without pause as they twist and turn in their perpetual hunt for often minute insects in total darkness.

As the day closes in, other animals wake up from their daytime retreats to resume their active lives. Some have made their homes in Rookery Wood while others are nocturnal visitors. During daylight you are unlikely to spot any, but occasionally you may be treated to the rear view of a fox as it dashes off into the undergrowth or a muntjac that has been disturbed from its daytime retreat in a thick bramble thicket – indeed there is one that has adopted the wood as its permanent residence. The best way to observe all these animals is to install infra-red sensitive trail cameras. By so doing I have discovered an unseen world of nocturnal activity – apart from foxes and our resident deer, I have recorded badgers which visit the wood every night, having burrowed under the wire fence, rabbits, wood mice running and jumping about, common shrews and one video record of a woodcock picking out grubs from under leaf litter.

Sadly night-time image quality from these cameras is appalling, producing monochrome images in which the animal is scarcely recognisable. Trail cameras work far better in daylight in my wood, when they capture a wide variety of common birds such thrushes, robins, pigeons, pheasants and a redwing, together with far too many grey squirrels. Occasionally though one is in for a real surprise. One image reveals a stoat dragging a rabbit over a ditch; another a buzzard having just caught a rabbit; and one, presumably the same bird, flying down a narrow woodland path with overhanging vegetation, far from a typical buzzard habitat.

[1] Most spider web is invisible to the naked eye (2.5-4 μm), unless coated with globules of moisture from the air or a sticky secretion produced by the spider. During spring and summer the webs are laden with 'gossamer' strands. These are usually made at ground level by so-called money-spiders (from the Linyphiidae family). As spring gives way to summer these webs are far less visible due to the sun being higher, so less back lighting and the drier air reducing condensation on the web.

[2] Greenhouse effect is a more descriptive term than the euphemistic one of global warming.

[3] Giant pond weed, *Potamegan natans,* is an invasive weed on Rookery Pond having almost entirely covered the surface during summer and thereby restricting the light penetrating to other plants and making it difficult for the visiting kingfisher to spot fish. During winter the leaves die and decompose at the bottom causing eutrophication and the built-up of silt.

[4] The web is so fine that it is virtually invisible to the naked eye, but I find the easiest way to find it is by either looking for the dimple where the web attaches to the water surface or the reflection of the spider in the water.

[5] see britishspiders.org.uk 'Notes on *Theridiosoma gemmosum*'

Wren

One of our smallest birds yet with one of the longest scientific names but its penetrating song and alarm calls more than make up for its diminutive size. Although basically a woodland bird, the wren *Troglodytes troglodytes* can be found wherever there is sufficient dense vegetation or low cover. Rookery Wood is ideal as there are so many piles of logs and coppiced material in which they can find invertebrate food and safe nesting sites.

The wren rarely flies more than a few feet off the ground.

Southern Hawker dragonfly *above*

Up to four of these large dragonflies have been known to set up separate territories around the pond, chasing one another when one wanders into the territory of another. They usually fly low and slowly around the water's edge, hunting for small flying insects, often coming to check you out within a foot or two. Their eyesight is legendary within the insect world, with up to 30,000 ommatidia (ie lenses) per compound eye.

Common frog *left*

Frogs are deservedly our most popular amphibian, probably due to their almost forward-facing limpid eyes. Here a common frog *Rana temporaria* surfaces from beneath a duckweed-covered patch of the pond for a breath of fresh air.

The moist skin of frogs allows them to carry on respiration for limited periods under water without using lungs, which during winter enables them to reduce their metabolism to tick-over and hibernate in the mud at the bottom of the pond, all the oxygen requirements being met by breathing through their skin.

For some reason, in Rookery Wood frogs are far less frequent that common toads.

Speckled bush cricket leaping

The speckled bush cricket *Leptophyes punctatissima* is commonly found in bramble thickets and nettle beds close to hedgerow and woodland borders. Unlike the majority of species in its family, this one is unusually quiet, capable of only weak chirps. The ears of bush crickets are located on their forelegs – a single hole with two eardrums.

The high speed set-up was originally intended for a hoverfly, but while looking for a suitable fly, I found this handsome cricket, so I took it back to the studio and promptly placed it on the fly's take-off perch. Much to my surprise and without delay, the insect leaped through the precise plane of focus, the depth of field being less than the width of the subject. The chance of this occurring is very remote. The insect was suitably rewarded with immediate release back to the wood.

Meadow grasshopper

Grasshoppers abound in the new meadow inside the fenced boundary immediately surrounding Rookery Wood. Free from grazing animals, this area has an expanding community of wild flowers and hence is alive with insects. The meadow grasshopper *Chorthippus parallelus* lives here alongside several other grasshopper species. One has been caught on a high-speed camera, a split second after take-off.

Green-veined white butterfly

Seen flying over a patch of creeping thistle, the green-veined white *Pieris napi* is by far the most common butterfly in this wood. On occasions I have seen up to ten flying around the large central glade at one time. Here, the caterpillar's food plants, cuckoo flower among several others, grow in abundance. When at rest, or captured in this instance by high-speed photography, the prominent green veins on the underside of the hind wings easily distinguish this butterfly from other whites.

Silver-washed fritillary in flight

I make no excuse for including four photographs of this spectacular butterfly, the silver-washed fritillary *Argynnis paphia*. Its presence in Rookery Wood justifies all the time and effort I have devoted in making the place ideal for this butterfly, a habitat with large trees, glades, rides and plenty of nectar-producing flowers for the adult – and dog violets for the caterpillars.

Silver-washed fritillary basking *above*

Laying eggs in the bark *below*

Silver-washed fritillaries mating

The various photographic techniques employed to capture these four pictures vary widely. The photo of the mating pair *(above right)*, a time when butterflies tend to be fairly placid, was a matter of simply being in the right place at the right time with the right lens. The specimen basking on a leaf of wild rose *(above left)* was a planned shot, taken by stalking the butterfly over an hour or so with a longish lens; whereas the shot of the female egg-laying *(left)* was a stroke of luck rather than genius on my part – the butterfly just settled in front of me at eye level when I had a suitable camera to hand. The high-speed photograph *(opposite page)* was another matter altogether. The picture may look simple, but it's the result of three or four days of painstaking preparation and photography after netting a specimen. The butterfly was released back into the wood after its accomplished performance – a final act that is always enjoyable.

71

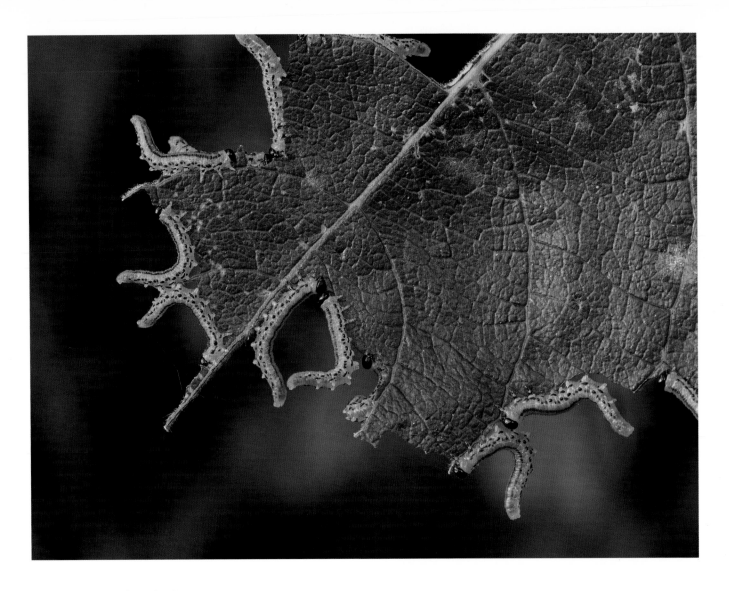

Lesser Birch Sawfly larvae

The activities of sawfly larvae are often made obvious by skeletonised leaves when only the veins remain, but the culprits have usually long gone. Here they are seen curled up at the edges of a leaf in an S-shape in typical sawfly fashion. This is the work of the lesser birch sawfly *Nematus pavidus*, in this instance feeding on a small willow growing at the pond's edge. The larvae of some species bore into fruits and stems. Sawflies possess two pairs of wings, like bees and wasps, rather than the single pair of flies.

Sawfly

This wasp-like insect is totally dependent on the water figwort on which its larvae feed. With its black and yellow bands, the figwort sawfly *Tenthredo scrophulariae* is an obvious wasp mimic and gains protection by being doing, but like all sawflies it is without a sting and completely harmless. Sawflies are not flies at all, but in the same order as wasps (*Hymenoptera*). Sawflies lack the narrow waists of bees and wasps and are considered to belong to a separate and more primitive group, *Symphyta*.

Water figwort *Scrophularia auriculata* has an attractive, tiny and easily-overlooked maroon-coloured flower and grows in abundance in Rookery Wood, providing a perfect habitat for this sawfly.

Roe deer *right*

A week or two after erecting the deer fence, I noticed fresh signs of damage to new coppicing shoots. It was clear that there had to be least one animal trapped in the enclosure. One evening about a month later while I was kneeling down photographing something at ground level, I became aware of movement to my right. On looking up I saw this delightful roe deer *Capreolus capreolus* walking up the ride towards me some thirty yards away. Having my camera to hand with a suitable lens attached, I gradually raised it to my eye and managed to expose a single image before the animal turned away and wandered off. Wildlife photography rarely works like this for me. Clearly the animal was not happy to spend its life stuck here, so I left a gate open overnight for it to escape and it was never seen again. Unlike fallow, roe are a rare sight here and then only seen singly or in pairs.

Fallow fawn saved from the blades *below*

Sometimes sentimentality takes precedence over ecological sense. One day while I was topping thistles immediately outside the deer fence, a fallow doe ran off from immediately in front of the tractor. I suspected that she had just given birth so jumped off to find a fawn a couple of yards from the front wheels gazing up at me with doleful eyes. Having my mobile to hand I took this snap.

Later in the day I contacted my friend Tim, who when not setting up flight simulators at Gatwick airport occasionally helps on my land and culls the deer. I

asked him to ignore the mother and fawn that he would almost certainly bump into while stalking. Over the following few months the pair were often seen peacefully grazing in the Holly Farm meadows. I try not to think about the number of offspring they spawned between them in subsequent years.

Hornet drinking sap from a fallen oak *above*

When the family first moved to Holly Farm in the 1970s there were no hornets at all. Now, probably thanks to the greenhouse effect, they are regularly found in Rookery Wood, their nests often discovered in hollow stumps, trees or holes in the ground; they are also frequent guests in our house. With their black and orange warning colouration and sinister buzzing flight, these insects sound menacing, but in reality they are very even-tempered, only stinging if severely provoked – though stirring up a hornet's nest is certainly not a sensible idea. This wasp is feeding on the sap oozing from a half dead oak tree that fell in the 1987 storm.

Red-tailed bumblebee *right*

The two most frequently-seen bumblebees in Rookery Wood are the buff-tailed *Bombus terrestris* and the tree bumblebee *Bombus hypnorum*. The red-tailed *Bombus lapidarius* is far less common here, but unlike some species with confusing brown bands, the queen and workers of this species are easier to identify with their jet black abdomen and bold red tail. This one has just taken-off from knapweed, a flower which is beginning spread well in some of the open areas of the wood.

Heron eating a frog *above*

Herons, *Ardea cinerea*, are very frequent visitors to this woodland pond throughout the year, as there is a rich source of prey here, including amphibians, sticklebacks and the odd dragonfly nymphs thrown in for good measure. One heron often roosts at night in an old oak close to the water's edge. This bird has just caught a juicy frog that was hiding in the shallows at the gloomier end of the pond.

Frosted orange moth *left*

The frosted orange, *Gortyna flavigo*, is a member of the Noctuidae family, a group of familiar and, at first glance, dull brown or grey moths with over 400 species in Britain. When examined more closely though, many of them, including the frosted orange, are attractively marked with subtle patterns and colours. This one is on the wing from late summer to October.

79

Long-jawed spider

This water-loving spider *Tetragnatha extensa* for some reason is not as common in this wood as it used to be. It is an attractive spider in both shape and colour, with a long tapered abdomen marked with light traces of silver, brown and green. Its cryptic pose of stretching out on a grass blade or twig with its eight legs stretched out in front and behind, can make it difficult to spot.

The spider constructs a delicate web with few radii and is set at 45 degrees or sometimes horizontally yet it is efficient at catching the flimsier waterside insects such as mosquitoes, midges and smaller mayflies.

Ray spider

The ray spider *Theridiosoma gemmosum* is a unique spider.
Once considered rare, this spider is extremely difficult
to spot, as apart from its diminutive size – not much
larger than a hefty full stop – it builds its web low down
in dark, damp corners a few inches above the surface of
the static water bodies of ponds and ditches. The web is
held in tension in the shape of a shallow cone rather like
an umbrella and is so fine that it is nearly impossible to see
unless backlit and covered with dew.

The most extraordinary thing is that this spider's flimsy web
is actually attached to the surface of the water at about two
points with a third point fixed to foliage at the water's edge.
I am proud to say that this fascinating behaviour was first
discovered by my colleague Evan Jones at this very site – a
man who has the most remarkable eyesight I have known.
He subsequently wrote a paper about his discovery for the
British Arachnological Society.

The easiest way to spot the spider is to look for its
reflection in the water rather than the spider itself.
Once more, Rookery Pond seems bristling with these
'rare' spiders.

Damselfly in flight *left*

The beautiful demoiselle damselfly, *Agrion virgo,* is an insect more reminiscent of tropical rainforests than Sussex woodlands. The male has an iridescent metallic blue body and ever-changing coloured wings of blue, green or brown depending on the light. The favourite haunts of this beguiling insect are stony-bottomed fast flowing streams where it spends its nymph stage. During courtship during May and June in places where they are common, dozens can be seen whirring in the dappled sunlight like miniature helicopters – a magical sight.

Thirty years ago this damselfly used to be reasonably frequent here, together with two other uncommon insects: the Giant crane fly, *Tipula maxima,* and Giant lacewingfly, *Osmylus fulvicephalus,* but now for various reasons including the arrival of the American signal crayfish which eats more or less anything that moves, it has all but vanished from my wood.

Toadlet resting on a floating foxglove flower *right*

By midsummer the seething mass of frog and toad tadpoles have developed four legs and are vacating the relative safety of the water for the perils that await them on dry land. In an effort to leave its aquatic habitat this one has clambered on one of the many foxglove petals floating on the water. For a day or two at this time of the year, the path around the pond is alive with these little creatures, making it almost impossible to walk without treading on them – so the family tries to keep away from the area then.

Scorpion fly

Scorpion flies (*Mecoptera*) frequent hedgerows and damp shady woodlands where they can often be seen resting on low vegetation waiting to pounce on a small sickly insect. They seem to have an almost indiscriminate appetite, moving from plant to plant on the lookout for dead or wounded insects, feeding on nectar, oozing sap or even stealing the contents from spiders' webs.

This male scorpion fly, probably *Panorpa communis*, is captured in flight, and shows its pointed beak and complex tail-end which is used for clasping the female when mating.

Bush-cricket

A female speckled bush-cricket, *Leptophyes punctatissima,* is grooming a foot while relaxing on the berries of tutsan, a type of St. John's Wort, *Hypericum androsaemum.*

White Admiral

The White Admiral reveals its stunning underside marked with subtle silvery-blue, brown, black and white hues, vying for subtle beauty with any other butterfly. The caterpillar feeds on honeysuckle and survives the winter by building a silken hibernaculum that remains attached to the food plant even after the plant has withered and died.

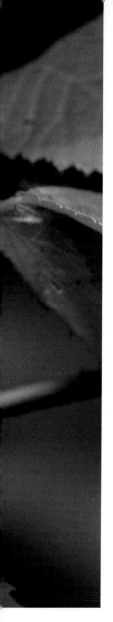

Gatekeeper

It is always a pleasure to see the first gatekeeper *Pyronia tithonus* or hedge brown as it is sometimes called when it first appears on the wing in July. Unfortunately though its flight period is rather short, lasting only about a month. The butterfly seems an approachable species and when not basking on a leaf, which it does a lot, it can be found feeding on various flowers especially bramble which grows so prolifically around the edges of the woodland's rides.

The gatekeeper has very variable wing colour and patterning and only the male has the dark bands across the fore-wing, as seen in this flight picture. It is easy to confuse this species with the meadow brown, the former having two small white pupils in the eyespots of the fore-wings. By comparison the meadow brown is a generally duller butterfly and prefers more open habitats like fields.

The woodland pond in June

A view of Rookery Wood pond taken early in its evolution.

To begin with there was no surface weed, only sedges and rushes, and little variety of marginal plants. Later the felling of alder and two large oak trees allowed more light and subsequent vegetation to become established. Excessive leaf-fall is also a problem when there are too many trees surrounding ponds.

Longhorn beetle in flight *left*

Longhorn beetles (*Cerambycidae*) are among the most impressive beetles found in Britain, or anywhere for that matter. They are often large and colourful and possess long antennae, sometimes longer than their bodies. Like most beetles, longhorns are clumsy flyers, this one crash-landing onto my arm as I was working in my wood. Needless to say this specimen was promptly captured and taken back to my studio for flight photography. The larvae of most longhorn beetles feed on wood, of which there is no shortage here.

Common carder bee *right*

Bumble-bees are among the first insects to appear in the year, sometimes even on the wing on sunny winter days. The attractive tawny brown carder bee *Bombus pascuorum* is one of the most common and easiest species to identify. Insects generally need warmth to fly, so how bumble-bees manage to become airborne in cold weather when almost all other insects are grounded and out of sight was a puzzle, until it was discovered that that they have the ability to effectively uncouple their wings from their flight muscles, allowing them to vibrate and warm up their thorax before flight.

During spring, the top end of Rookery Wood is humming with carder and buff-tailed bumble-bees taking advantage of the megastore of nectar provided by the acre or two of bluebells.

Greylag geese taking off

Over the last few years a pair of greylag geese, *Anser anser*, fly onto Rookery Pond with the intention of nesting on the island. Naturally all my family become excited at the prospect of seeing a bunch of fluffy little goslings splashing about on the water, but so far we have been disappointed. Most years these birds succeed up to the point of egg-laying, but some predator manages to plunder the eggs before the gosling have had a chance to take to the water. Recently the goslings managed to hatch and survive in the water for a few hours before mysteriously vanishing overnight, together with their parents. Whether the culprit was a crow, fox or mink I never discovered – or perhaps the whole goose family decided to leave the area for a safer home.

AUTUMN

AUTUMN is a time of transition as we move slowly from summer to winter, the season of mists and mellow fruitfulness when chlorophyll is broken down and its component parts are transported to the roots and stored for the following season. Some colours of autumn have been in the leaves all along. Over summer they have been masked by the green chlorophyll, but as the green is absorbed, the countryside transforms into beautiful shades of brown, yellow and red leaving the sugars and yellow-orange pigments to play at rainbows. Days are shortening and temperatures are dropping, yet for many, this is the best time of the year. The fervent bustle, growth and breeding activity of spring and summer is over and nature needs time to wind down.

When viewed from a distance, many temperate woodlands develop into a mosaic of varying colours at different speeds, depending on tree species and their distribution. Rookery Wood, although not the most visually impressive wood at this time of the year, is made up largely of English oak, a tree which, together with ash, displays browns rather than the brighter colours of beech *Fagus sylvatica* or maple. Fortunately the wood has a scattering of field maple *Acer campestre*, a tree that turns bright yellow in late autumn.

As autumn advances, the variety of wild flowers diminishes but those that remain such as ivy *Hedera helix,* water mint *Mentha aquatica* and hemp-agrimony *Eupatorium cannabinum* tend to be quite prolific in Rookery Wood. Ivy climbs many trees and stumps, particularly those near edges of the wood or glades which benefit from more light, and by late autumn the ivy flowers are literally humming with all manner of insects, particularly hoverflies *Syrphidae* and wasps, including those magnificent insects, hornets. Butterflies, especially those preparing to hibernate like red admirals *Vanessa atalanta* and peacocks feast on the generous supply of nectar produced by ivy, and others like the comma *Polygonia c-album*, large white *Pieris brassicae*, and an occasional holly blue *Celastrina argiolus* are not infrequent guests. Water mint grows in profusion in the central part of the wood, thriving anywhere that is sufficiently wet like the pond edges and the number of ditches of running water. Hemp-agrimony is another lover of moist places. It is a tall plant with frothy pink flowers throughout a long flowering season, attracting a large range of insects from the older silver-washed fritillaries of late summer to the many autumnal insects including the peacock butterfly *Aglais io* and a wonderful variety of hoverflies.[1]

Autumn is the time when the woodlands and hedgerows bear fruit such as blackberries *Rubus*, rose hips *Rosa canina*, haws (from hawthorn *Crataegus monogyna*), elderberries *Sambucus negra,* sloes (from blackthorn *Prunus spinosa*) and crab apples *Malus*. All these appear in Rookery Wood at some time during autumn and all provide a supplement for various bird and mammal visitors. Signs of their autumn diet in the form of undigested fragments of fruits or purple stains is evident in the droppings from these animals.

Many of the adult insects that were prominent during the summer months have now disappeared and been replaced by the next generation in egg, larval or pupal form, hidden out

Yellow Stagshorn *far left*

The bright yellow stagshorn, *Calocera viscosa,* is a particularly striking fungus which is occasionally found in the wood growing on old conifer stumps.

Yellow Brain fungus *left*

Another bright yellow fungus is the yellow brain, *Tremella mesenterica.* Oddly, it is parasitic on another fungus (*Peniophora*) which grows on hazel.

Southern Hawker dragonfly

The inquisitive southern hawker *Aeshna cyanea* and the emperor dragonfly *Anax imperator* are the largest dragonflies which spend their lives as adults and nymphs, in and around Rookery Pond. When at rest, their cryptic colouration makes them difficult to spot but once airborne, they take on a new dimension, which after 300,000 years of evolution enables these spectacular insects to perform any aerobatic manoeuvre including flying backwards, sideways or even inverted for short periods, in their pursuit of insect prey.

of sight and harm's way. Among the larger insects still active at this time of the year are the late brood butterflies such as the peacock and red admiral and a few species of dragonflies that are on the wing in the vicinity of the pond. By far the commonest is the common darter *Sympetrum striolatum*, a busy insect that's on the wing until the end of October when it can be prolific. It is fiercely territorial, the red males chasing off anything that flies near them. Meanwhile the southern hawker dragonfly remains on the wing well into November, surviving the early frosts to be seen on the dullest autumn days patrolling the pond edges at head height in its hunt for small insects.

Rookery Wood is blessed with interesting spiders. Unfortunately these eight-legged creatures are not popular with some but their fascinating lives and subtle and sometimes stunning colouring imbues them with a beauty of their own. A drawback is that most species are too small to be noticed. Like so much wildlife, many spiders are especially attracted to woodland borders and water, habitats that are ideal for insects on which they depend. Among the larger species is the striking marbled orb weaver which is rare or absent over much of the country, but found locally in some parts of Sussex including this woodland. Another early autumn medium-sized spider is the boldly-marked bordered orb weaver *Neoscona adianta*, by no means common. Other more common spiders live all over the wood but especially in the central zone where there is plenty of water and light, for instance the familiar garden or cross spider *Araneus diadematus*. It lives in similar habitats to the marbled orb weaver. By far the most frequently-seen species are the lesser garden spider, *Metellina segmentata,* and the long-jawed spider, *Tetragnatha extensa.* The latter is a slim tapering species with long fine legs and outsized chelicerae (jaws). One of my favourite spiders is Britain's largest jumping spider, the so-called fence spider, *Marpissa muscosa,* a species with a long season from summer to October. It is an impressive little beast capable of prodigious jumps and although not common, it frequents the margins of Rookery Wood where it hides under the loose bark of trees or fence posts supporting the fence. During warm sunny weather this spider is tempted out of its lair to bask on an old branch as it waits for prey to land within jumping distance.

Another creature you may love or hate is the grass snake, *Natrix natrix*, a delightful reptile that goes into hibernation in October because, like other reptiles, it is unable to function properly when its body temperature becomes too low. Fortunately there are plenty of places where it can hide such as the numerous 'bug piles' of litter from coppicing and strimming that have deliberately not been removed. Less fortunately, grass snakes have plenty of predators that regularly visit the wood such as foxes, badgers and herons. During autumn there is little or no bird song apart from the robin which sings all the year round, its autumn song particularly sweet and melancholy. There are several robins thriving here, one of which usually hovers around to take advantage of any disturbance caused by my management activities and so keeps me company. The rooks are intermittently noisy especially in the evenings, when they assemble prior to leaving to roost elsewhere, though where they go is a bit of a mystery.

Fungi are everywhere in woodlands. The complex symbiotic relationship between plants and fungi is little understood but we do know that it is fundamental to the lives of all healthy forests the world over. Without these fascinating life forms, the forests, their inhabitants and ourselves would not survive long. Fungi are beneath our feet, in the air and on almost every surface we set eyes on. The mushrooms and toadstools that we are familiar with are a mere glimpse of their true bodies which branch throughout the medium on which they live. The collective name for the white fungal hyphae is mycelium. This network can be seen underneath the bark of rotting tree stumps or under leaves of a damp forest floor. The hyphae produce enzymes to aid the release of nutrients which are absorbed together with water from the medium in which they grow.

Because it is damp and rich in fallen wood and leaves, Rookery Wood supports a wide range of fungi from the notorious honey fungus, *Armillaria,* that thrives on sickly trees, stumps

Mycelium

Without mycelium the world would not exist as we know it. Mycelium is the vegetative part of fungus, the part that fungi are all about. The fruiting body, the bit we see, is only a small part of the organism. Mycelium is made up of masses of thread-like hyphae which produce enzymes that help the fungus to absorb nutrients from its host. It somehow connects up to all the trees through this network of fungal threads. This seems to play a major but mysterious part in the 'communication' within the woodland plant community.

and roots to the minute fungi that are scarcely visible. Some of these so-called fungi are classified as slime moulds – which are not moulds, fungi, animals or plants, but soil-dwelling collections of amoeba-like masses consisting of hundreds of thousands of cells. Slime moulds are certainly mysterious forms of life that are even capable of very slowly creeping about like giant amoebae. They commonly inhabit woodlands and enhance the diverse life in Rookery Wood.

[1] There are nearly 300 species of hoverflies in Great Britain, many of which mimic wasps or bees. Their mouthparts have evolved to suck the nectar from flowering plants and their presence aids pollination. They are all entirely harmless and add variety and beauty to the fauna of our countryside.

Moorhen

A pair of moorhens *Gallinula chloropus* nest on the pond every year without fail. Like herons, moorhens are extremely shy birds, going into panic mode as soon as they catch a glimpse of a human, certainly on this pond anyway, when the birds fly off to completely vanish into the bogbean or marginal vegetation.

I find it difficult to get excited by moorhens as all they seem to do is to swim about lethargically, pecking at the odd bit of pondweed. And my feelings for these birds is hardly enhanced by any photographs I take of them on the pond, as the water surface is always very messy with small rafts of green algae or weed to distract the eye!

Peacock butterfly

The peacock, *Aglais io,* used to be a common butterfly in Great Britain, but alas, like so many butterflies, over the years its numbers have diminished. Peacocks are lovers of gardens, visiting all sorts of nectar-producing flowers such Michaelmas daisies and buddleia. Usually these striking insects appear in the wood during autumn visiting hemp-agrimony, and later, on ivy flowers when in bloom.

Like other members of its family (Nymphalidae), peacocks are fast and powerful flyers. The late brood even stays with us during winter when they hibernate in hollow trees, piles of logs, old buildings and sheds, appearing again in spring to breed.

Fungus

With so much rotting wood and damp areas in Rookery Wood, fungi have a field day here. From left to right, we have the collared parachute, *Marasmius rotula*; sulphur tuft *Hypholoma fasciclare*; and what is probably a *Psathyrella sp.*

Fence Spider

Jumping spiders, *Salticidae,* catch insects by leaping onto them, often stalking their prey, cat-like from several inches away. Two headlight-like high resolution forward-facing eyes (they have six others) have the unique ability of focussing, as far as I know, by moving the retina, helping them to have more acute eyesight than any other spider *(see detail below).*

The fence spider *Marpissa muscosa* is Britain's largest jumping spider, living in cracks and crevices of fences or under the bark of dead or dying trees, especially those exposed to warm sun. It is extremely well camouflaged, so unless moving, very difficult to spot.

The spider is by no means common but can be found locally in certain areas in the southern part of the UK. The easiest place to find them in Rookery Wood is on the peeling fence posts on a hot summer or early autumn day.

Kingfisher

Ever since the pond was excavated in the mid 1990s, there have been regular visits from this spectacular bird during the summer and autumn months. Originally there were no fish here so I introduced a jar-full of 3-spined stickleback, *Gasterosteus aculeatus,* taken from a friend's lake – perfect fodder for attracting the kingfisher, *Alcedo atthis,* but not so dominating as to demolish all the aquatic invertebrates. After all, it is insects that make a body of water alive and interesting rather than a bunch of large mud-stirring fish!

To encourage the bird to the best spot I set an old oak branch deep into the clay pond base at the edge of a six foot deep trough which I thought would be a perfect habitat for the fish and provide a suitably unfussy background for my photography.

In this photograph I avoided a fancy high-speed shot of the bird diving into the water – preferring to show the kingfisher at ease within the tranquility of its lovely habitat. As it was such an irregular visitor, many hours over several days were spent in the natural hide made from coppiced branches. Waiting in hides over long periods can tax one's patience, but not so here with so much insect and bird activity surrounding me.

A woodland glade for the Speckled Wood

The dappled light of this woodland glade in autumn is the perfect spot to see the speckled wood butterfly *(see below)*.

An interesting feature of the speckled wood, *Pararge aegeria,* is that – uniquely among British butterflies – it has the ability to overwinter as either caterpillar or pupa. The butterfly has two or even three broods a season and so is on the wing from April to September.

It is fiercely territorial, chasing off any intruders that appear in its home patch.

Marbled-orb weaver spider *far left*

The best places to find the web of large and handsome marbled orb weaver *Araneus marmoreus* web is near the pond and around the brambles and lower branches of surrounding trees. Because the spider spends much of its time hiding in a silken retreat close to vegetation, it is easier to find the large orb web rather than the spider itself, although it can be gently coaxed out for viewing. This spider is quite a scarce species in most of the country but a relatively frequent species in this part of Sussex.

Bordered-orb weaver spider *right*

Another attractive and largish spider occasionally found in this wood is the bordered orb weaver *Neoscona adianta*. On a couple of occasions I have found it positioned in the centre apertures of the wide-gauged perimeter fence.

The web-like limbs of a dead tree *centre*

The top portion of Rookery Wood can be classified as ancient woodland as it has much larger trees than the lower regions and a number of indicator plants such as dog's mercury and wood spurge. It also has plenty of dead trees, many at ground level which are best left to continue their life-cycle and benefit the rest of the wood for decades by supplying nutrients to the younger trees as they decay. At the same time they support many other life-forms such as insects, mites and springtails, fungi and bacteria, all vital for the overall ecology of the wood, as they rot .

Robin

The sweet melancholy song of the robin, *Erithacus rubecula,* is especially evident during autumn evenings when most other birds have fallen silent.

The males are notorious for their aggressive behaviour towards other males, defending their territory with vigour and have even been known to fight to the death.

Yet the cock bird shows the touching trait of feeding his mate, about the only way of distinguishing between the otherwise identical sexes.

Grass snake

With the colder weather of late autumn, the grass snake *Natrix natrix* is ready to escape from the winter, but like other snakes it does not hibernate in a true sense but brumates, when it finds a hole underground or under a tree and slows down its metabolism until the temperature rises again in spring.

Rookery Pond in autumn *right*

Although this photograph was taken in mid-October, you wouldn't think it. Most of the trees around the pond are not known for their brilliant autumnal colours. A subtle shift in the saturation of the greens is probably the best way to describe this tranquil scene.

Pipistrelle bat emerges from under the rafters

A late evening visit to Rookery Wood during summer and autumn months will almost always be rewarded by the sight of bats, largely pipistrelles *Pipistrellus pipistrellus* flying above the pond in their perpetual hunt for the rich supply of small aquatic-based insects that live here. Video from the trail cameras also reveals very blurred evidence of bats flying down the narrow wooded paths. Plainly, this picture was not taken in the wood, but of a bat flying from the eaves of my barn close-by where several dozen bats roost during the day (I have counted up to 36 leaving from a single entrance).

The barn, which also happens to double as my studio, and is only a couple of minutes from my wood, is the home for dozens of these fascinating mammals, so there can be little doubt as to where the bats visiting the wood have originated from.

Hazel Dormouse

Although there is strong evidence to support the presence of dormice *Muscardinus avellanarius* in Rookery Wood today, I have been unable to photograph them here for the simple reason that it is illegal to capture or interfere with these threatened mammals in any way. This photograph was taken of a local dormouse in the 1980s, when such regulations did not apply. With the thick growth of dense scrub and developing hazel coppice, this wood is ideal for these charming mammals, so the image could not be omitted!

Although dormice have the reputation of being very slow and dozy, they can put on a surprising turn of speed and even jump well when the need arises. These animals go into deep hibernation from November to April.

Hoverflies

There are nearly 300 species of hoverfly in Britain, many of which are mimics of bees or wasps, but all of course are utterly harmless. Here are four of them (clockwise from top left): *Eristalis pertinax, Eristalis sp., Helophilus pendulus* (tiger hoverfly) and *Eristalis arbustorum*.

Fox

Foxes, *Vulpes vulpes,* are either loved or loathed – I belong to the former category, never ceasing to be thrilled whenever I see one wandering around the fields here, or in this instance strolling down a narrow, overgrown path in the wood catching the last of the evening sun. It was a lucky shot – I noticed the fox approaching about 70 yards away, so I crouched behind a patch of brambles and waited for it to appear through a narrow gap. Fortunately, I was returning from an attempt at photographing the elusive kingfisher, so I had the perfect lens to capture this magical moment.

Brimstone butterfly

The brimstone, *Gonepteryx rhamni,* can be seen in Rookery Wood right up until late September. This butterfly was found superbly camouflaged hiding under a hazel leaf. Even the rust spots on the leaf seem to be mimicked on the brimstone's underwing.

Although typically a woodland insect, it is found in a range of habitats including gardens and hedgerows. The brimstone wakes up from hibernation during the first warm days of April, the brighter male first, followed by the paler female a week or two later. At a distance the female brimstone can be mistaken for the large cabbage white, but the brimstone has a more direct flight.

Rhinoceros beetle

The rhinoceros beetle, *Sinodendron cylindricum,* is sometimes referred to as the least stag beetle (not to be confused with the lesser stag beetle – another species entirely!) It is most likely to be encountered in woodlands because its larva feeds on the wood of dead trees. Although widespread, it is not a common insect. This is the only specimen I have found here and it is such an impressive insect that it had to be recorded 'on film'.

Rooks assembling

Every evening the rooks, *Corvus frugilegus,* assemble on a dead oak tree close to the edge of the Rookery Wood, then, just before sundown, they all take off with much commotion to roost somewhere else. But as yet, I know not where.

Blue-tits

Although blue tits, *Cyanistes caeruleus,* can be found in a wide range of habitats including gardens, they are essentially woodland birds where there is generally a greater abundance of live food for feeding their young than in gardens. During winter they search for seeds and buds and insects and other small invertebrates that are concealed in tree stumps and other nooks and crannies.

WINTER

〰〰〰〰〰〰〰〰〰〰〰〰〰

IN COMPARISON with the rest of the year, winter seems dead in Rookery Wood, with hardly any movement or sounds apart from the rooks and a few birds flitting about in the trees. Bird song is absent, there is no sound of rustling leaves overhead, or the hum of insects to draw one's attention, yet unobtrusively, life is ticking over in the background.

After all the activity of spring and summer, trees need a rest. Signs of wear and tear were already showing at the end of summer when the lush greens had started to fade with tinges of softer yellow-browns showing at the edges of leaves. In some ways trees and other plants can be compared with animals that need to build up fat reserves before going into hibernation such as dormice, bats and some larger mammals like the bears of colder continents of the north. Trees may not fatten up with nuts and berries or salmon, but fuel up they do, in the form of energy from the sun and chlorophyll gained during the summer months which is used to make sugar and other compounds. All these bio-chemical processes are stored in the roots and trunk together with the broken-down compounds of chlorophyll that are available for the formation of buds and leaves for the following spring. But only when the leaves have drifted down to ground is the tree ready for winter.

Slime mould

The weirdest organisms in the wood are slime moulds – living things which are neither animals, plants nor fungi. They generally consist of a huge single cell with thousands of nuclei, which are formed when individual flagellated cells fuse together, so forming a bag of cytoplasm with multiple nuclei. There are three groups of slime moulds all with life-cycles superficially resembling fungi and they come in all manner of shapes, sizes and colours. They live in moist habitats such as decaying wood or cow dung. This specimen, an *Arcyria sp* was discovered under the bark of the anti-deer fence posts.

Rookery Wood still shows signs of the winter storm of 1987 in the form of fallen trees, especially at the top end of the wood where many of the trees were unusually still in leaf – another good reason why deciduous trees lose their leaves in winter. When in leaf, a large tree has a surface area of about 1,000 square yards, which in a 60mph gale generates a force equivalent to about 200 tons – enough to damage the tree or even blow it down. This danger is amplified when the roots are in saturated soil as they find it harder to gain purchase, but as winter is normally the season for gales and heavy rain, the absence of leaves significantly reduces the risk of damage. It is also worth noting that nature has designed trees to bend like the wings of aircraft, distributing the powerful aerodynamic forces more evenly throughout the trees' structure. The power of the wind and the massive strength of trees is compellingly demonstrated when watching a large tree swaying in a gale – the same source of power that is capable of raising a 500-ton jumbo jet into the air.

Wild flowers are virtually absent during winter. One plant which does blossom from time to time in Rookery Wood, brought on no doubt by our warming winters is herb robert *Geranium robertianum*, a type of crane's-bill, which can occasionally be seen in full flower as late as December. Another plant is lesser celandine *Ficaria ficaria* which only occurs in small numbers around moist spots such as on the banks of the stream. It is one of the first flowers to appear in late winter and a welcome sign that spring is on the way. Primroses *Primula vulgaris* start flowering in February and in Rookery Wood they grow in profusion on the banks and drier rides.

Because much of the wood is quite damp, it is home to many mosses, lichens and liverworts that festoon the boles and branches of blackthorn and some of the larger trees. These tiny plants date back to before the dinosaurs and thrive during winter when in the absence of leaves they are more conspicuous.

During the heat of summer insects are everywhere, but as soon as it becomes cold and frosty they seem to vanish completely, only to reappear mysteriously in spring. They have adopted a number of techniques to avoid the cold altogether. The most straight-forward approach is to simply avoid the cold by flying to somewhere warmer. In Britain some butterflies and moths return to Mediterranean countries from whence they may have come – painted ladies and silver-y moths (*Autographa gamma*) for example, both of which are visitors to Rookery Wood. Other insects make it through winter by hibernating as adults, while some butterflies including red admirals and brimstones hibernate in hollow trees, ivy thickets or in the wood's gardening cabin. The majority of insects survive as eggs, larvae or pupae, hiding in cracks and crevices or by burrowing deep underground away from frosts. Aquatic insects wait out the winter at the bottom of the pond where they can remain relatively comfortable even when the water freezes, others such water beetles or water bugs do this as adults, while dragonflies and mayflies and their kin do so as nymphs.

Birds on the other hand do not benefit from all these options. They either fly off to somewhere warmer or see the winter out here. Rookery Wood birds such as thrushes, robins, wrens and tits are just as active in the wood during winter as they are at other times although many insect-eating birds like the blackcap and chiffchaff have moved on to warmer parts of the world. But to compensate there are also winter visitors such as redwings, *Turdus iliacus,* which I hear more often than see. Surprisingly, even some of the wood's blackbirds may be winter visitors from the continent as not

Ravens

There have been a pair of ravens *Corvus corax* living in the valley for over ten years now and they can be seen flying directly over Rookery Wood almost every day. Their unmistakeable deep croaks mean that they are generally heard before seen; this couple is playing against the clear blue winter sky, their characteristic wedge-shaped tails and the 'heavy' front end makes them difficult to confuse with other corvids.

all are native. When wandering 'off-piste' during winter, I often disturb a woodcock, *Scolopax rusticola,* which springs into the air almost at my feet and flies off, zigzagging between the ash trees. They are so well-camouflaged that there is little hope spotting them until they take to the air. Woodcocks are peculiar birds as they are active at night when they search among the ground litter for invertebrates – I haven't any pictures, but have a blurred trail camera video taken at night of one poking about in leaves with its long bill. Unfortunately they are becoming increasingly rare.

The larger mammals, having squeezed under the tough wire fence, stalk around Rookery Wood every night, as evidenced by the trail cameras. Badgers are particularly determined animals and will stop at nothing to gain access to almost anywhere, borrowing under the fence with their powerful claws. Stoats, *Mustela erminea,* and the occasional brown rat, *Rattus norvegicus,* have been caught on camera too. Wood mice, *Apodemus sylvaticus,* are very common and to a lesser extent, the bank vole, *Clethrionomys glareolus* also puts in an appearance. On the rare occasions when it snows, the activities of both these little mammals under the insulating blanket of snow can sometimes be tracked by locating the dark patches where they surface from time to time.

Finally we come to the grey squirrel, *Sciurus carolinensis*, an animal which I would prefer to forget. This animal trips the camera trap during daylight more frequently than any other creature. Endearing though grey squirrels may look, these aliens are far too common in Rookery Wood; in reality they are nothing more than tree rats, raiding birds' nests and eating their eggs and young, not to mention pilfering every one of the thousands of hazelnuts, leaving next to nothing for any dormice that may be living here, let alone for my family! Regrettably, I have done little to control the numbers of this pest, partly because I prefer carrying a camera or scythe to a gun.

Herb Robert

This little pink flower, herb robert *Geranium robertianum*, also known as cranesbill, storksbill and a number of other local names has a very long season from March to well into winter. It is common in many parts of the world and pops up in all sorts of shady spots in this wood. The plant is reputed to contain powerful anti-oxidants and various vitamins, providing health-giving properties including boosting the immune system and treating cancer.

Rookery Wood stream in winter flood

Unfortunately the lower part of the wood which includes the stream could not be fenced off due to the topography of the land. As a result deer accumulate in wildebeest-like herds eroding the ground and the stream banks as they wander back and forth. Unfortunately there are no crocodiles to control them!

To make matters worse the stream has been invaded by another alien, the signal or American crayfish *Pacifastacus leniusculus*. The creatures not only burrow into the bank below the water line, resulting in collapsing banks, but are also responsible for killing off much of the aquatic fauna, including fish (mostly brown trout in this case) and insect larvae such as the beautiful demoiselle dragonfly *Calopteryx virgo*, one of the most beguiling insects found in Britain.

A wood mouse emerges from its mossy hole

Although the wood mouse (also known as the long-tailed field mouse), *Apodemus sylvaticus*, is rarely seen during the day – my trail camera videos show these hyperactive little rodents hopping about all over the wood in gay abandon every night, recording their activities almost anywhere the camera is positioned. Daytime is spent hiding away under logs and stumps, but by twilight they are out to raid their stores of seeds and berries buried in underground burrows.

Rather than truly hibernating, the wood mouse goes into a torpid state but resumes normal life during warm winter spells, although there are signs of its activity even when there is snow on the ground.

Rookery Wood under winter mist

A drone photograph taken on an early winter morning with mist drifting down the valley at the bottom of Rookery Wood. The tall evergreen trees are Douglas firs (see overleaf) – these relatively young specimens stand out clearly above the rest of the canopy.

This photograph was taken by my son Lee using our jointly-owned drone.

Douglas Fir

The fifteen or so Douglas firs, *Pseudotsuga menzeisii,* which are dotted around the wood, unlike all the deciduous trees, grow up dead straight and have lost many of their lower branches. Only the peg-like remnants of earlier branches remain. This tree can grow well over 200 feet high and live for about 1,000 years.

Visitors to Rookery Wood caught by my trail camera

Clockwise from top left: 1. Badger rootling around for slugs or snails at base of tree 2. Suspicious fox peering at trail camera 3. Buzzard about to fly off with a rat caught on the narrow woodland path 4. Fox hunting on wooded path at twilight 5. Stoat dragging rabbit over ditch 6. Muntjac breaking into my wood under the newly-erected fence.

16-spot ladybirds *left*

I came across this small bunch of orange 16-spot ladybirds, *Tytthaspis sedecimpunctata,* hibernating among a pile of hazel logs on a cold winter's day while coppicing. The beetle is considered an indicator of ancient woodland, and was once common on sycamore trees, but it recently transferred its attention to ash trees as well, so it should thrive well here. Interestingly this ladybird feeds on mildew fungus.

Bracket fungus *right*

This particularly fine specimen of the polypore bracket fungus, *Trametes multicolor,* is visually at its best during autumn and winter. Polypores are a group of fungi that, rather than having gills on the underside of their fruiting bodies, have pores or tubes containing the spores.

The species, found on dead or dying hard woods such as oak and ash, is extremely variable in colour. It is described as being uncommon.

Rookery Wood pond in winter

With the insidious march of global warming, snow is a rare event in mid Sussex these days. On this occasion, I must have been up early enough to catch the snow on the branches before it had a chance to melt or blow off.

Lichen and moss

All the trees in this woodland are splattered with a colourful variety of lichens and mosses. These strange growths are not single organisms but a stable symbiotic association between fungi, algae and/or cyanobacteria, bacteria that obtain their energy through photosynthesis. They come in a wide range of colours, sizes and forms.

Liverwort

Liverworts, *Bryophyta,* not to be confused with lichens and mosses, are non-vascular flowerless spore-producing plants. The spores are produced in small capsules, often with supporting stalks. Several of the wet banks of the steams and ditches in the wood have dark green patches of liverworts – this one is the Common Liverwort, *Marchantia polymorpha*, which has a worldwide distribution. The word 'wort' simply means small plant.

Signs of winter's end and spring's beginning

For me, the sight of blackthorn blossom drifting though the wood like cloud is among the most beautiful signs of early spring. It comes at a time when there is very little colour in the wood apart from a few unfurling green leaves. As is clear from the photograph, Rookery Wood, thanks to the exclusion of deer, is thick with an almost tropical growth of vegetation – loved by so many creatures. I am just waiting for nightingales to arrive now!

Fallow deer, seen from a drone, in a field beside my wood

If these things had the run of Rookery Wood all hell would break loose! This is a comparatively small herd by normal standards around this part of Sussex, as there are others over twice this size. Fallow deer are really browsers rather than grazing animals. If they kept to grazing the fields there would be no problem, but once they get into woodland, over time they will destroy almost every bit of greenery whether wild flower or sapling that dares to show its face above ground. Even impossibly prickly plants like bramble and blackthorn are in the for chop!

MANAGING
ROOKERY WOOD

WOODS, like gardens, evolve with time – and like gardens they require planning and maintenance to thrive, especially if maximum benefit to wildlife is the primary aim. Some see woodlands in pure monetary terms while others enjoy them simply as places to romp around in. Woodmanship such as coppicing can make a profound ecological improvement to a wood; often it's the unexploited woods that deteriorate and disappear. It is very unfortunate for our diversity that modern technology and the use of plastics has helped to eliminate sustainable timber, traditional crafts and local jobs. It has resulted in many woods becoming overgrown with a permanent high and dense canopy, thus excluding the light needed by woodland flowers and wildlife

This section is not intended as a general guide to woodland management. Rather, it outlines some of the steps I adopted to extend the range of animals and plants that lived in or visited my wood. My priorities are not necessarily those of other woodland owners, so other types of woods may well require a different approach.

Most of Rookery Wood was planted over a hundred years ago for future timber extraction and probably for sporting purposes such as fox hunting or pheasant shooting. Heavily wooded with ash together with some oak and old hazel, it was dark and far from ideal for wildlife which requires woodland with open spaces and edges, one of the most important features. Woodland edges are the interface between open ground and the large forest trees, and is the area where there is maximum light. Ideally the plant heights should gradually increase from ground level to the taller trees, providing a shrubby intermediate layer, thus encouraging a diverse range of plants. In this way the whole ecology of the wood benefits.

As most trees grow slowly, the ash and oak were unlikely to provide a quick return, but hazel is much quicker so could have been expected to start generating some earlier cash by traditional woodland management; indeed it is clear that the hazel was coppiced sometime during the mid 20th century. By practising traditional woodland crafts, our wood-loving ancestors may well have been the first conservationists, preserving not only the trees, but enhancing the richness of the surrounding woodland plants and wildlife. Coppicing would have been at the centre of these activities, and is done before the sap rises, in late winter and early spring.

Coppiced hazel

Three years after the protective fence was erected we started coppicing. Rabbit damage is reduced by cutting to about 2ft above ground. Soon an understorey developed of fresh hazel, seen here in autumn with young yew, bramble and wild flowers lining the path, all providing cover, nesting sites and food for the local wildlife.

The principle of coppicing is to harvest the growth that sprouts out from a cut-down tree or stool as it has now become – the harvest cycles varying from 7 to 20 years. In this way wood is produced for different purposes, depending on its length and thickness – for hedge-laying, beanpoles, hurdles and logs.

Perhaps more than any other woodland activity, it is coppicing that promotes the greatest biodiversity. It should also extend the life of the tree many times over. Ideally there should always be areas of coppice (coupes) that are coppiced in different years, thus providing a range of stages of height and habitats for a wide variety of wildlife including small mammals like dormice and nesting sites for birds. At the same time the extra light reaching the forest floor encourages wild flowers to germinate, and invertebrates to thrive. As a result the whole ecosystem blossoms in a coppiced woodland. Hazel is excellent for most traditional crafts, while ash is ideal for open fires and wood burning stoves, and its larger timber such as the trunk is perfect for making furniture, planks and cricket bats.

Rookery Wood is too small for producing traditional woodland products in any serious way apart from the felled ash which is used for logs and planks. The brushwood and smaller branches from coppicing are stacked up to form 'bug piles' which are dotted around throughout the wood. These piles provide a haven for all manner of bugs and are popular with wrens, robins and small mammals which live or roost in them.

When I bought the wood in the late 1980s, its habitat was far from ideal for wildlife. As most of the area was covered in ash trees and neglected hazels that had not been coppiced for decades, very little light was able to penetrate down to the forest floor. Furthermore the ground flora was dominated by that thug of a plant, pendulous sedge. It became clear the whole wood desperately needed opening up through a programme of felling and coppicing.

Pendulous sedge
Before the erection of the deer fence.

The first task was to cut a meandering path to allow easy access for machinery into the whole area. Simultaneously, to relieve the gloomy interior and encourage fresh vegetation especially woodland flowers, I

An early experiment

Before taking the plunge of fencing the entire woodland, I conducted a test where a small area was fenced off with some temporary plastic fencing. This photograph shows the dividing line between the two sides of the fence, only 2 or 3 years after erection. The foreground is for all intents and purposes dead. No argument!

began felling ash in the central zone and coppicing hazel on the north side. Surely with more flowers attracting more invertebrates, the larger animals should follow? Sadly however, over the next couple of years the coppicing proved to be a complete waste of time and effort – the fresh growth from the hazel that I and my helpers had so enthusiastically coppiced was being demolished by fallow deer, ultimately resulting in dead stools – plants cannot survive long without leaves! What started out as a few alluring 'bambies' dotted around the landscape, in the fullness of time became an insidiously increasing plague that wrought havoc almost everywhere they roamed. Massive holes appeared in hedges and the modest variety of wild flowers that grew around their margins vanished. At the same time what little ground flora that had sprung up in both Rookery Wood and the surrounding woodlands was being stripped bare by their activities – not to mention the fate of the stools.

I had failed to appreciate the terrible damage herds of deer can wreak in woodland and also their capacity to breed like rats! Stalking had little or no effect: one would be shot while the remaining several dozen would gallop off into the wood. I was flummoxed. Short of calling in the army or a helicopter gunship, the only logical solution was to surround the entire woodland with a two-metre high anti-deer fence, an option I could ill afford at the time.

Before throwing in the sponge entirely I was offered a free length of 2-metre high plastic fencing. Although this would not survive large falling branches and the determined efforts of badgers and rabbits for long, it was worth experimenting with a couple of hundred yards of the stuff

148

around a limited area. Within two seasons this little patch of Rookery Wood took on a new lease of life with wild flowers springing up and modest growths of brambles – and the coppiced stools had grown six foot high shoots. Even insects were flying about in the sunnier spots. The experiment left me in no doubt that the entire woodland had to be protected with a proper galvanised wire deer fence. With finances already stretched I applied for a Forestry Commission grant. It was not long before Forestry officials arrived on the doorstep to inspect the place. They made encouraging noises, one reflecting my feelings by describing it as a potential mini-paradise – praise indeed from a government official! The following season, having gained a modest grant from the Forestry Commission, the full nine-acre wood was fenced.

With buoyed spirits, I lost little time in embarking on a more radical programme to enhance the wildlife potential of Rookery Wood by creating more and larger glades. Potentially the most exciting area was the centre zone which contained a stretch of bog. This consisted largely of patches of dark peaty water with an abundance of alder, *Alnus glutinosa*. As it appeared to hold water throughout the seasons, it seemed a good plan to transform the bog into a proper woodland pond, so I hired a JCB, grubbed out much of the alder and some of the surrounding trees. A good omen from the start was the arrival of a kingfisher *Alcedo atthis*, which landed on the bucket of the digger while the operator was having a nap although it did not appear again until the following summer.

Constructing the deer fence

Building the full fence around the 9-acre woodland took two men about a fortnight to complete. Most of the holes for the posts were made with a tractor-mounted post borer (auger), but where the ground was sufficiently soft, the posts were simply hammered into the ground by this machine. In some places, due to hard seams of sandstone or tree roots, the 2½-foot deep holes had to be dug by hand.

Creating a glade

The centre of the wood which consisted largely of ash trees and sedge was the best area for creation of a large glade. I felled about 70 trees, so allowing far more light to penetrate thereby encouraging a much wider variety of vegetation. In the long term, this bold plan will pay dividends.

The making of a woodland pond

Shortly after excavation, this half-acre woodland pond had already started to fill by natural springs. Once filled, the water depth varied from about six inches in the shallows to six feet in the centre.

The resulting half-acre pond (which my kids call the lake!) varied in depth from 6 inches to 6 feet, and now, thanks to the more open canopy, sunlight is able to fall on most of the water and its margins for much of the day. Although the pond was created in a summer, by late autumn it had filled thanks to an active spring and looked as though it had been established for years. The capacity of nature to recover, at least at ground level, is remarkable, as fresh greenery sprang up from bare rutted areas within a few weeks.

Particularly exciting was the water's magnetic ability to attract wildlife, aided in the case of Rookery Wood by being free from undue disturbance by humans or pollution from agricultural chemicals. My pond was not used for boating, water-skiing, exercising dogs or the breeding of duck and geese, any of which can spell disaster for a small patch of water. Within days of filling, insects such as pond skaters, water boatman and dragonflies appeared from seemingly nowhere – it was almost as though, like the kingfisher, these insects had been hovering over the area during its construction waiting for the crater to fill. Within a year mallard, herons, moorhens, visiting kingfishers and various mammals including on one single occasion the rare water shrew *Neomys fodiens* were spotted. Each season the water's edge is decorated with various wild flowers including ragged robin *Lychnis flo-cuculi*, lady's smock *Cardamine pratensis*, primrose *Primula vulgaris*, water figwort *Scrophularia auriculata*, water mint *Mentha aquatica*, water Dropwort *Oxypolis filiformis* and kingcups *Caltha palustris*, all of which serve to attract a range of insects. Additionally two large introduced patches of bog bean *Menyanthes trifoliata*, are now providing low-level secluded perches for emerging damsel and dragonflies and thick cover for moorhens and other water birds.

Many of the basic changes to the structure of Rookery Wood have now been completed but general maintenance is a never-ending activity. The rides and glades require topping or scything while the narrower trails and the perimeter track around the pond are kept clear of bramble and pendulous sedge by strimming. The pond itself, although not without its problems from accumulation of giant pond weed, more or less looks after itself in the medium term, but fallen branches and debris from strimming and scything need dragging out from time to time.

Although brambles provide wonderful habitats for insects and nesting birds, they grow extremely rapidly and require frequent cutting back during the height of the season. With this in mind I tend to wander about the wood armed with a unique home-made long-handled chopper in one hand (and often a camera in the other). By maintaining a razor-sharp edge to the blade I can slice through any brambles, pendulous sedge, nettles or other over-enthusiastic plant by a mere flick of the wrist – without having to bend down!

Wrecked hedge

Thick healthy hedges act as wildlife corridors allowing smaller creatures, especially mammals, to travel along and populate small woods relatively safely under cover. Unfortunately many of the hedges in the vicinity of Rookery Wood have over the years been severely browsed by fallow, breaking the efficiency of these links. They don't look too good either.

Developing the meadow inside the deer fence

When the full fence was finally erected, I deliberately retained a 50-100ft grassy space between the wood's borders and the fence. Now, thanks to the absence of fallow, it is developing into a healthy meadow area. This picture was taken only two years after its erection.

The wood is seen on the left and in the background, and the fence on the right. Just visible in the distance are marsh thistles, white clover, and a large and expanding area of bird's foot trefoil (yellow). There are also several other flowers together with small saplings of oak and ash which don't show here. In turn this new habitat attracts a wide range of insects including various bees, several grasshopper and bush cricket species, butterflies such as blues, skippers, and even silver-washed fritillaries.

Beyond the fence (top right) is only grazing grass used by deer, with virtually no insect life. If evidence is ever needed to show the enormous damage fallow do to biodiversity, you don't have to look any further than here.

SOME OF THE SPECIES IN ROOKERY WOOD

Mammals
Badger *Meles meles*
Bank Vole *Myodes glareolus*
Brown Rat *Rattus norvegicus*
Fallow Deer *Dama dama*
Field Vole *Microtus agrestis*
Fox *Vulpes vulpes*
Grey Squirrel *Sciurus carolinensis*
Hazel Dormouse *Muscardinus avellanarius*
Mole *Talpa europaea*
Muntjac, Reeves *Muntiacus reevesi*
Pipestrelle Bat *Pipistrellus pipistrellus*
Rabbit *Oryctolagus cuniculus*
Roe Deer *Capreolus capreolus*
Stoat *Mustela erminea*
Water Shrew *Neomys fodiens*
Wood Mouse *Apodemus sylvaticus*

Reptiles and Amphibians
Common Frog *Rana temporaria*
Common Lizard *Zootoca vivipara*
Common Newt *Lissotriton vulgaris*
Common Toad *Bufo bufo*
Grass Snake *Natrix natrix*
Palmate Newt *Lissotriton helveticus*
Slow-worm *Anguis fragilis*

Birds
Barn Owl *Tyto alba*
Blackbird *Turdus merula*
Blackcap *Sylvia atricapilla*
Blue Tit *Cyanistes caeruleus*
Bullfinch *Pyrrhula pyrrhula*
Buzzard *Buteo buteo*
Canada Goose *Branta canadensis*
Carrion Crow *Corvus corone*
Chaffinch *Fringilla coelebs*
Chiffchaff *Phylloscopus collybita*
Coal Tit *Periparus ater*
Goldcrest *Regulus regulus*
Goldfinch *Carduelis carduelis*
Great Tit *Parus major*
Great-spotted Woodpecker *Dendrocopus major*
Green Woodpecker *Picus viridis*
Greylag *Anser anser*
Grey Wagtail *Motacilla cinerea*

Heron *Ardea cinerea*
Hobby *Falco subbuteo*
House Martin *Delichon urbicum*
Jackdaw *Corvus monedula*
Jay *Garrulus glandarius*
Kestrel *Falco tinnunculus*
Kingfisher *Alcedo atthis*
Linnet *Carduelis cannabina*
Long-tailed Tit *Aegithalos caudatus*
Magpie *Pica pica*
Mallard *Anas platyrhynchos*
Mandarin *Aix galericulata*
Marsh Tit *Poecile palustris*
Mistle Thrush *Turdus viscivorus*
Moorhen *Gallinula chloropus*
Nuthatch *Sitta europaea*
Pheasant *Phasianus colchicus*
Raven *Corvus corax*
Redwing *Tardus iliacus*
Robin *Erithacus rubecula*
Rook *Corvus frugilegus*
Siskin *Spinus spinus*
Skylark *Alauda arvensis*
Song Thrush *Turdus philomelos*
Sparrow Hawk *Accipiter nisus*
Swallow *Hirundo rustica*
Swift *Apus apus*
Tawny Owl *Strix aluco*
Tree Creeper *Certhia familiaris*
Woodcock *Scolopax rusticola*
Wood Pigeon *Columba palumbus*
Wren *Troglodytes troglodytes*

Butterflies and Moths
Brimstone *Gonepteryx rhamni*
Comma *Polygonia c-album*
Frosted Orange Moth *Gortyna flavago*
Gatekeeper *Pyronia tithonus*
Green-veined White *Pieris napi*
Holly Blue *Celastrina argiolus*
Large White *Pieris brassicae*
Large Skipper *Ochlodes sylvanus*
Orange-tip *Anthocharis cardamines*
Painted Lady *Vanessa cardui*
Peacock *Aglais io*
Red Admiral *Vanessa atalanta*
Silver-washed Fritillary *Argynnis paphia*

Silver Y Moth *Autographa gamma*
Small Skipper *Thymelicus sylvestris*
Speckled Wood *Pararge aegeria*
White Admiral *Limenitis camilla*

Dragonflies
Azure Damselfly *Coenagrion puella*
Banded Demoiselle *Calopteryx splendens*
Beautiful Demoiselle *Calopteryx virgo*
Blue-tailed Damselfly *Ischnura elegans*
Broad-bodied Chaser *Libellula depressa*
Brown Hawker *Aeshna grandis*
Common Darter *Sympetrum striolatum*
Downy Emerald *Cordulia aenea*
Emperor *Anax imperator*
Large Red Damselfly *Pyrrosoma nymphula*
Southern Hawker *Aeshna cyanea*

Other Insects (among myriads of unidentified species)
Alder Fly *Sialis lutaria*
Bee Beetle *Trichius fasciatus*
Bee Flies *Bombyliidae*
Bumble Bees (various)
Caddisflies (various) *Trichoptera*
Cardinal Beetle *Pyrochroa serraticornis*
Common Carder Bee *Bombus pascuorum*
Common Wasp *Vespula vulgaris*
Craneflies (various) *Tipulidae*
Figwort Sawfly *Tenthredo scrophulariae*
Giant Cranefly *Tipula maxima*
Giant Lacewing *Osmylus fulvicephalus*
Green Lacewing *Chrysopa spp.*
Honeybee *Apis mellifera*
Hornet *Vespa crabro*
Hoverflies
   Eristalis tenax
   Eristalis arbustorum
   Helophilus pendulus
   Sphaerophoria scripta
   Catabomba pyrastri
   Syrphus spp.
   Myathropa florea
Lesser Birch Sawfly *Nematus pavidus*
Lesser Stag Beetle *Dorcus parallelipedus*
Longhorn Beetle *Strangalia maculata*
Long-legged Flies *Dolichopodidae*

Mayfly *Ephemeroptera vulgaris*
Meadow Grasshopper *Chorthippus parallelus*
Parasitic Flies *Tachinideae spp.*
Rhinoceros Beetle *Sinodendron cylindricum*
Scorpion flies *Mecoptera spp.*
Scorpion Fly *Panorpa communis*
7-Spot Ladybird *Coccinella septempunctata*
16-Spot Ladybird *Tytthaspis sedecimpunctata*
Speckled Bush-cricket *Leptophyes punctatissima*
Wasp Beetle *Clytus arietis*

Some Spiders

Angular-Orb Weaver *Araneus angulatus*
Bordered-Orb Weaver *Neoscona adianta*
Crab spider *Diaea dorsata*
Fence spider *Marpissa muscosa*
Four-spot Orb Weaver *Araneus quadratus*
Funnel Web spider sp. *Coelotes terrestris*
Garden spider *Aranea diadematus*
Hammock Web Weaver sp. *Lyniphia triangularis*
Lesser Garden Spider *Metellina segmentata*
Long-jawed spider *Tetragnatha extensa*
Marbled-Orb Weaver *Araneus marmoreus*
Nursery-Web spider *Pisaura mirabilis*
Ray spider *Theridiosoma gemmosum*
Wolf spiders (various species) *Lycosids spp.*

Plants

Bird's-foot Trefoil *Lotus corniculatus*
Blackberry *Rubus spp.*
Bluebell *Hyacinthoides non-scripta*
Bogbean *Menyanthes trifoliata*
Bulrush (Reedmace) *Typha latifolia*
Bugle *Ajuga reptans*
Buttercup *Ranunculus spp.*
Centaury *Centaurium erythraea*
Cleavers *Galium aparine*
Common Liverwort *Marchantia polymorpha*
Common Spotted Orchid *Dactylorhiza fuchsii*
Cowslips *Primula veris*
Creeping Thistle *Cirsium arvense*
Dock *Rumex crispus*
Dandelion *Taraxacum officinale*
Dog Violet spp. *Viola riviniana*

Dog's Mercury *Mercurialis perennis*
Early Purple Orchid *Orchis mascula*
Enchanter's Nightshade *Circaea lutetiana*
Forget-me-not *Myosotis sylvatica*
Goosegrass *Galium aparine*
Giant Pondweed *Potamegon natans*
Golden Saxifrage *Chrysosplenium oppositifolium*
Ground Ivy *Glechoma hederacea*
Gypsywort *Lycopus europaeus*
Hedge Woundwort *Stachys sylvatica*
Hemp-Agrimony *Eupatorium cannabinum*
Hemlock Water-dropwort *Oenanthe crocata*
Herb-Robert *Geranium robertianum*
Honeysuckle *Lonicera periclymenum*
Horsetail *Equisetum arvense*
Ivy *Hedera helix*
Kingcup *Caltha palustris*
Lesser Celandine *Ficaria verna*
Lady's Bedstraw *Galium verum*
Lesser Knapweed *Centaurea nigra*
Lesser Spearwort *Ranunculus flamula* Lesser
Stichwort *Stellaria graminea*
Lady's Smock (Cuckoo-flower) *Cardamine pratensis*
Lords-and-Ladies (Cuckoo-pint) *Arum maculatum*
Marsh Thistle *Cirsium palustre*
Opposite-leaved Golden Saxifrage *Chrysosplenium oppositifolium*
Oxeye Daisy *Leucanthemum vulgare*
Pendulous Sedge *Carex pendula*
Primrose *Primula vulgaris*
Ragged Robin *Lychnis flos-cuculi*
Red Campion *Silene dioica*
Red Clover *Trifolium pratense*
Scarlet Pimpernel *Anagallis arvensis*
Selfheal *Prunella vulgaris*
Sow Thistle *Sonchus arvensis*
Speedwell *Veronica spp.*
St Johnswort
    Hypericum perforatum (Perforate)
    Hypericum officinale (Tutsan)
Tutsan *Hypericum androsaemum*
Water Dropwort *Oxypolis Filiformis*
Water Figwort *Scrophularia auriculata*
Water Mint *Mentha aquatica*

Water-plantain *Alisma plantago-aquatica*
White Clover *Trifolium repens*
Wild Daffodil *Narcissus pseudonarcissus* Wild
Rose *Rosa canina*
Rosebay Willowherb *Chamerion angustifolium*
White Dead-nettle *Lamium album*
Wild Garlic (Ramsons) *Allium ursinum*
Wood Anemone *Anemone nemorosa*
Wood Avens *Geum urbanum*
Wood Spurge *Euphorbia amygdaloides*
Wood Sorrel *Oxalis acetosella*
Yellow Pimpernel *Lysimachia nemorum*
Yellow Iris *Iris pseudacorus*
Yellow Archangel *Lamiastrum galeobdolon*

Trees

Alder *Alnus glutinosa*
Ash *Fraxinus excelsior*
Beech *Fagus sylvatica*
Blackthorn or Sloe *Prunus spinosa*
Crab Apple *Malus sylvestris*
Douglas Fir *Pseudotsuga menziesii*
Elder *Sambucus nigra*
English or Pedunculate Oak *Quercus robur*
Field Maple *Acer campestre*
Hazel *Corylus avellana*
Hawthorn *Crataegus monogyna*
Holly *Ilex aquifolium*
Japanese Cedar *Cryptomeria japonica*
Silver Birch *Betula pendula*

Crusteaceans and Molluscs

Amerian Signal Crayfish *Pacifastacus leniusculus*
Banded Snail *Capacea spp.*

Fungi

Yellow Stagshorn *Calocera viscosa*
Yellow Brain *Tremella mesenterica*
Honey Fungus *Armillaria spp.*

Fish

Three-spined Stickleback *Gasterosteus aculeatus*